Family Business Blueprint

Generational Wealth, Creative Family Collaboration
And A Lifestyle Legacy

Liz Zed

Published by Vividly Visioning Publishing

1182-H Pacific Rim Hwy, P.O. Box 402

Tofino, British Columbia, V0R 2Z0 Canada

ISBN: 978-0-9950160-4-0

Dedication

For my mum Ruby and my brother Bill who taught me that family is everything and Always comes first.

Acknowledgments

Celebration of 40 years in business 2024!

With sooo much gratitude

Our amazing team past and present.

My business partners

You're simply The BEST! You've taught me so

much. We wouldn't be where we are today

had it not been for YOU. I AM so grateful

40 years of customers Wowza!

You have been Amazing

Thank You

Contents

Introduction - Starting A Business In The Middle Of Nowhere With No Money And No Skill

My journey as an entrepreneur started in the midst of uncertainty and struggle. It was a beautiful day at the beach, where my family and I had built a small cabin after making the bold decision to leave the big city and our professional careers behind and embrace a back-to-the-land lifestyle in a quaint village at the edge of an ocean. We had always dreamed of dedicating our time to raising our children together, surrounded by nature and simplicity. However, our dreams were quickly met with the harsh reality of financial strain. Despite our best efforts and our agreements prior to leaving the city that one day we might have to take on jobs again, we agreed in advance that it would have to be part time positions only, for each of us, so that we could dedicate a serious chunk of free time to family life. Unfortunately, I hadn't been able to find a suitable part-time job, and neither had my children's dad. After a months-long employment search he finally was offered a full-time position which he accepted as a "temporary measure", just to keep the lights on and the bills paid. Ultimately, that full-time job demanded a lot of his time away. We found ourselves in a situation where we were working long days separately, he at work on the other end of the peninsula, and I at home with two wee ones and the responsibilities of motherhood. We were beginning to realize that each of us were feeling like we were no closer to achieving our ideal family life.

The turning point in our journey came when we realized that we needed to take matters into our own hands. We were tired of feeling like we were just surviving, and we wanted to create a future where we could thrive as a family. It was then that we made the bold decision to start a family business, despite having little to no money or previous experience in entrepreneurship. I was determined to find a business idea that would not only be financially viable but would also align with our values and bring joy to our community.

As we embarked on the journey of starting a family business, I faced another unexpected obstacle. My husband, always a devoted dad, decided to step back from our plan, leaving us both half-time single parents with two young children and separate lives. My dream then seemed more daunting than ever. But I refused to let fear or doubt hold me back. I poured my heart and soul into building a family business anyway, meeting with local regulators, and conducting a year-long market test to ensure that the idea had potential.

When the time came for a grand opening, I felt a mix of excitement and nerves. I was facing the unknown as a single parent and an entrepreneur, but I knew that this was my chance to create a better future for my family. It was a sink or swim moment, and I chose to swim with all the strength and determination I could muster.

Eventually, the little business took off, and it was incredibly rewarding to see the positive impact it had on our small town. Over time, this family business helped turn our village into a thriving destination. Both of my children grew up participating in the business and during their teen years both become my business partners and began to assume huge leadership roles with responsibilities equal to, and eventually surpassing even mine. We worked together to build a successful family legacy that continues to thrive today. Our family legacy now includes the active participation of my two eldest grandchildren.

Looking back on our journey, I've come to realize that pursuing the ideal lifestyle and manifesting our dreams is a continuous process. It's about looking for opportunities in the face of obstacles, and understanding that the pursuit of a family business can bring fulfillment, creative freedom, and financial stability. Our story is a testament to the fact that with perseverance, passion, and a commitment to our shared vision, a family business can be the catalyst for a life filled with purpose and joy. So to all the beginner entrepreneurs out there, I urge you to embrace the challenges, stay true to your values, and never underestimate the power of a dream shared with your loved ones.

I hope my story can inspire you to create the lifestyle of your dreams and if that dream includes having a family business you'll find some ideas to think about as well as encouragement here. We can begin with a couple of questions.

Are you tired of the 9-5 grind and longing for financial freedom and independence? Have you ever considered the idea of starting a family business? If you have dreams of creating a lifestyle where you can work on your own terms, have more quality time with your loved ones, and leave a lasting legacy for future generations, then a family business could be the answer you've been searching for.

Say Goodbye To The Constraints Of A Traditional Job And Hello To Being Your Own Boss.

One of the greatest benefits of creating a successful family business is the freedom it provides. Running a family business allows you to take control of your financial future and live life on your own terms.

Flexibility is another key advantage of running a family business. With flexible working hours, you'll have more time to spend with your family and pursue the things that matter most to you. Imagine being able to attend your child's school events or take a family vacation without having to ask for time off.

In addition to personal freedom, a successful family business can create a legacy of generational wealth. Building a thriving business provides the opportunity to secure financial stability and prosperity for your children and grandchildren. It's a way to ensure that your family is taken care of for years to come.

Working together in a family business can also bring you closer to your loved ones. Through shared values and a common purpose, your family unit can become stronger and more connected. The experience of working towards a shared goal can create lasting bonds and a sense of unity among family members.

Involving family members in the business can instill a strong work ethic and entrepreneurial spirit that will evolve as you grow and continue in future generations. It's a chance to pass down valuable skills and knowledge, setting the stage for continued success and growth in the family business.

In addition to fostering a strong work ethic, running a family business can improve communication and understanding among family members. As you work together towards a unified vision and common goals, you'll learn to communicate effectively and support one another through both challenges and successes.

Financial security is another important benefit of having a family business. With a stable source of income, you can provide for your family's needs and enjoy peace of mind knowing that you have a reliable source of revenue.

Furthermore, the collaborative nature of a family business can inspire creativity and innovation. Working with your loved ones can lead to new business ideas and opportunities, as you share your different perspectives and ideas. It's the perfect environment for nurturing creativity and pushing the boundaries of what's possible. Watch and be amazed as your entrepreneurial offspring expand and creatively branch out with their individual endeavours even as they remain firmly rooted in family entrepreneurship!

Last but not least, successfully running a family business can strengthen family bonds and create lasting memories of shared achievements and successes. As you celebrate milestones and overcome challenges together, you'll create a legacy of resilience, achievement, and unity that will last for generations to come.

In conclusion, starting a family business can be a rewarding endeavor that provides financial freedom, family creativity and bonding, a lifestyle that reflects your values, and an enduring family legacy. By working together towards common goals, families can create a strong and sustainable business that not only supports their financial needs but also fosters strong family connections. With a focus on shared values, a strong work ethic, and creativity, a successful family business can leave a lasting legacy for future generations. Whether it's a small local business or a larger venture, the benefits of starting a family business are numerous and can lead to a fulfilling and meaningful lifestyle for all involved. If you've ever dreamed of a lifestyle where you can work with your loved ones, make a difference, and leave a lasting impact, then a family business could be the key to making those dreams a reality. So why wait? Start building your family business today and unlock the potential for a future of financial freedom, creativity, and lasting family legacy.

From Dream To Reality: Crafting A Family Business That Transcends Generations

Creating a successful family business that not only provides financial freedom but also fosters family creativity, connection and a lasting lifestyle legacy with generational wealth is a dream that many of us aspire to achieve. However, the journey to achieving this dream can be both exciting and daunting. This is the crucial reason why I created a blueprint for you to work from, as you embark on this rewarding endeavor. So, if you are ready to begin, let's lay the blueprint out on the table and take a look at what you'll be building.

The first main step in this process involves defining the family business concept and mission. Bring the family together to brainstorm potential business ideas, aligning them with each family member's skills and interests. By doing this, you are not only ensuring that the business is a true reflection of your family's collective talents and passions, but you are also setting the stage for a successful venture standing on a strong foundation.

Creating a detailed business plan, which is the second main step, is critical for mapping out the path to success. It sets the framework for identifying the target market, developing a marketing and sales strategy, and determining the initial investment and funding sources. A well-thought-out business plan not only guides you in the right direction but also instills confidence in potential investors and partners. As a bonus, you might also gain some insight into your personal money mindset in the process. Or, at the very least perhaps initiate some curiosity that could turn you in the eventual direction of invaluable self-awareness.

Establishing a solid legal and financial foundation, followed by building a strong brand and online presence, are fundamental for laying the groundwork for a successful family business. These main steps ensure that your business is legally compliant, financially secure, and has a strong and recognizable presence in the market.

The implementation of effective marketing and sales strategies, the cultivation of a positive company culture, and planning for sustainable growth and succession are subsequent main steps that are equally crucial in maintaining and growing your family business. These steps foster collaboration, innovation, and continuous improvement, while also ensuring a smooth transition for the business to prosper for future generations.

By following the steps outlined in this book, you will be well on your way to creating a family business that not only provides you with financial freedom but also allows you to nurture family creativity, connection, and a lasting lifestyle legacy. It is my hope that this book serves as an indispensable guide for anyone looking to achieve generational wealth and a thriving family business for years to come.

Dream Big, Think Family: Defining Your Business Mission

This chapter will help you:

- Generate potential business ideas by involving your family in a brainstorming session to identify skills, interests, and hobbies that can be turned into a business opportunity.

- Research market trends and potential customer needs to ensure that the business idea is relevant and in demand within your community.

- Agree on the mission and values of your family business by aligning business goals with your family's values and vision, creating a strong foundation for the business.

- Decide on a business name and logo that reflects your family's mission and values, ensuring that the brand is memorable and representative of what your business stands for.

- Utilize tools and resources such as borrowing materials from friends, seeking input from others, creating checklists, and compiling relevant resources to guide and inspire you through this critical step in defining your business mission.

Embracing The Unknown: How A Single Mom And Her Kids Built The Ultimate Family Lifestyle Legacy

It was a long and challenging journey for me, as I tried to navigate my way through the complexities of starting a family business. I was a mother of two young children, just trying to find a way to create a source of income that wouldn't take me away from them. I longed for a lifestyle that allowed me to be present for my children while also pursuing my entrepreneurial ambitions. But with no clear idea of what business to start, I found myself lost and uncertain about how to proceed.

I had been working as an academic researcher, but the stress of city life and a taxing job in child protection had taken a toll on me. I longed to escape the burnout and vicarious trauma, and devote myself to creating a nurturing and healing environment for my children, full of love, creativity, and joy. However, despite my longing for a change, I was at a loss about what business venture to pursue.

Everything changed one day when my next-door neighbors invited me to try out their new surf gear. As I ventured into the ocean, I experienced an overwhelming sense of renewal and joy. It was an experience that filled my soul and brought me a sense of fulfillment I hadn't felt in awhile. That's when it hit me - everyone should have the opportunity to experience this kind of joy and freedom.

From that day on, I began taking my 4-year-old son to the beach every day while his baby sister napped in the red flyer wagon, nestled in blankets at the water's edge. The sense of peace and happiness I felt during those moments was indescribable. It was as if the universe had answered my prayers, and I was filled with a newfound sense of purpose and determination.

I knew I had to make this work. I had a vision of creating a business that would bring this same sense of joy and adventure to others, while also allowing me to provide for my family. The path ahead seemed daunting, but I was determined to pursue my dream.

As I delved into the details of bringing my vision to life, I realized that the first step was to find a name that represented my values - love, fun, adventure, health, and nature. It was essential to me that the name would inspire me and resonate with my vision. I also needed to create a logo that captured the essence of what I wanted to share with the world. It was a daunting task, but I was determined to bring my dream to life.

As I began to spread the word about my vision, I found an outpouring of support and resources that I never expected. It seemed as though the universe was aligning to help me make my dream a reality. I found an artist who could create a logo that perfectly reflected the spirit of my business, and I was overwhelmed by the generosity and willingness of others to help me on this journey.

It was in this moment that I realized the beginning stages of starting a family business requires a deep dedication to a dream, as well as a willingness to create a vivid vision of what you truly want. As I juggled the implications of each decision, I came to understand that every choice somehow referred back to what would work best for my children and I. Aligning my values with my goals and being creative with my options allowed me to make choices that were perfect for me and my family.

Even from the beginning, it seemed, I was being taught lessons that creating a family business is not just about building a source of income, but about crafting a lifestyle that aligns with your values and allows you to create the life you want for your family. It's about finding a way to pursue your passion and provide for your loved ones while staying true to yourself. As I reflect on my journey, I now understand that the decisions I made were all part of creating a life that works for me, hopefully served and will continue to serve my children, and my children's children, as they choose the path that's best for them going forward! Looking back on this decades-long journey from today, I am filled with gratitude for the opportunities that have been and those that lie ahead.

Now, it's your turn to create and manifest your vivid vision and have Fun!

Here, I will help you define the concept and mission of your family business. This is an important step in building a strong foundation for your business, so let's get started.

Step 1: Generate Potential Business Ideas.

You can approach this as an exciting and fulfilling process because it can be. Encourage open and creative thinking. To kick things off, gather your family together and have a brainstorming session. Ask each family member to share their skills, interests, and hobbies, and to focus on what's inspiring and fun. For example, if your family loves baking and cooking, you might consider a business related to catering, starting a food truck, or even opening a family-run restaurant. Perhaps your family loves gardening and taking care of plants, and you might consider a business related to landscaping, plant care, or a plant nursery. Is your family full of talented designers and artists? Perhaps an interior design agency would suit you.

Another potential business idea could stem from your family's shared love for crafting and DIY projects. Perhaps you could explore the possibility of starting a handmade jewelry business, creating and selling custom home decor, or even opening an online store for homemade candles and soaps.

If your family enjoys spending time outdoors, consider a business related to outdoor adventures or activities. This could involve starting a family-owned outdoor tour company, offering guided hiking or camping trips, or even opening a small local gear supply shop. Embracing your family's love for the great outdoors can lead to a business venture that brings joy and fulfillment to each member.

Should your family have a fondness for animals, you might explore the idea of starting a pet care or grooming business. This could involve offering pet sitting services in your neighborhood, opening a doggy daycare, or even launching a mobile pet grooming service. Doing what you love while caring for animals can be a rewarding and uplifting experience for the whole family.

Ultimately, the key to generating potential business ideas is to tap into your family's unique skills, interests, and passions. **Embrace the collaborative spirit, and encourage everyone to share their creativity and insights.** The options are endless when it comes to building a family business that aligns with your collective passions and interests. By exploring different avenues and thinking outside the box, you'll be one step closer to building a family business that reflects your collective dreams and aspirations.

Step 2: Research Market Trends And Potential Customer Needs.

After generating a list of potential business ideas, it's important to research market trends and potential customer needs. Take the time to understand the industry you're entering and how you can best serve your community. This might involve talking to people in your local area, conducting online research, or even attending industry events to gather insights.

Step 3: Agree On The Mission And Values Of Your Family Business.

Once you have a clearer understanding of the potential business ideas and the needs of your community, it's time to agree on the mission and values of your family business. This step involves aligning your business goals with your family's values and vision. For instance, if your family values environmental sustainability, your mission might focus on providing eco-friendly products or services and/or stewardship and responsibility towards the planet.

Other Ideas For Brainstorming Family Values:

- Providing high-quality products and services that prioritize customer satisfaction and meet the needs of your community, in line with your family's commitment to integrity and excellence.

- Fostering a positive and inclusive work environment that values teamwork, respect, and open communication, reflecting your family's belief in the importance of collaboration and empathy.

- Supporting local charities and community initiatives through donations and volunteer work, in keeping with your family's values of giving back and making a positive impact in the world.

- Honoring your legacy of entrepreneurship and innovation by continuously seeking new opportunities for growth and adaptation in the ever-changing business landscape, in line with your family's vision of embracing change and striving for long-term success.

- Finally, you may want to consider the logistics of location and time, and the impact of these on how you will be together as a family at work and at home. How might these aspects be configured as an optimum reflection of your values?

Step 4: Decide On A Business Name And Logo.

Lastly, it's time to decide on a business name and logo that reflects your family's mission and values. The name and logo should be memorable and representative of what your business stands for. Consider involving all family members in this process to ensure that everyone feels connected to the brand. You might want to keep your branding ideas in the foreground during this process of setting up your new family business as it can be a critical component. You may want to revisit and revise as you go until you get it right, or adjust it over time.

To Help You Through This Process, Consider Using The Following Tools And Resources:

- *Create a vision board.* Get creative with a family afternoon vision board session. Schedule a couple of hours of family time and gather all the materials: poster boards, coloured pens, a stack of magazines, scissors, glue stick, glitter, etc. Either have each family member create their individual board and share with each other when complete, or you can collaborate on creating one vision board. Never underestimate the power of visualizing. Vision boarding is especially fun and effective when done the old-fashioned way (with the materials described above vs using a computer program with a limited digital image selection). You're just more present at the cellular level! AND it doesn't hurt to spend a few minutes in quiet contemplation before you start, to prime the pump of the receptive brain and get creative juices flowing. Don't let people tell you vision boarding doesn't work. It's worked for me and hundreds of clients over the years. I've used this practice to great success in group vision boarding sessions, even with hardened criminals in court mandated, residential treatment facilities, and the joy and transformation that occurred over subsequent months with productive action and dreams realized is something extra special to behold!

- *Borrow materials from friends*. If you're exploring a new hobby or trying out a potential business idea, consider borrowing materials from friends to minimize initial costs.

- *Try things if you don't know what you like.* Don't be afraid to experiment and try new things. Sometimes, you might discover a passion you didn't know you had.

- *Ask for input.* Seek input from friends, family, and mentors who can provide valuable perspectives and feedback.

- *Checklist of basics.* Create a checklist of basic steps to ensure that you're covering all aspects of defining your business mission.

- *Additional list of resources that could be helpful.* Compile a list of resources such as books, websites, or workshops that could provide guidance and inspiration.

Remember, defining your business mission is an important part of the journey towards creating a successful family business. Take the time to involve your family in this process and ensure that the mission and values align with your collective vision. Got your creativity cap on yet? Are you having fun? Good luck!

Chapter Summary

> ➤ Generate potential business ideas through a family brainstorming session

> ➤ Research market trends and potential customer needs in the industry

> ➤ Agree on the mission and values of your family business that align with your family's vision

> ➤ Decide on a business name and logo that reflects your family's mission and values

> ➤ Utilize tools and resources such as creative vision boarding, borrowing materials, trying new things, seeking input, creating checklists, and compiling helpful resources to aid in the process. Stay tuned for the next chapter.

Chapter FAQ

Question: *Why is it important to align the mission and values of the family business with the family's own values and vision?*

Answer: It's important to align the mission and values of the family business with your family's own values and vision because it ensures that the business is a reflection of your family's principles and beliefs. Perhaps you haven't put too much time into considering your values. As a coach, I can tell you that trouble happens going after goals that don't align with your values! If defining values is a new process for your family, this is an excellent time to start. Values alignment creates a sense of authenticity and helps to build a strong connection between the family, the business, and its customers. For example, if a family values environmental sustainability, their business mission might focus on providing eco-friendly products or services.

Question: How can a family ensure that their business mission and values are authentic and meaningful?

Answer: A family can ensure that their business mission and values are authentic and meaningful by staying true to their core beliefs and principles, being genuine in their messaging and practices, and consistently demonstrating their values through their actions and business decisions.

Question: What are some common mistakes to avoid in the process of defining the family business mission?

Answer: Some common mistakes to avoid in the process of defining the family business mission include not involving the entire family in the decision-making process, overlooking market research and customer needs, and not aligning the business mission and values with the family's own beliefs and vision.

From Vision To Reality: Mastering The Art Of Business Planning

This chapter will help you:

- Identify your target market and customer demographics to tailor your products or services to meet their specific needs.

- Develop a marketing and sales strategy that is aligned with your target market's preferences and behaviors.

- Determine the initial investment and explore potential funding sources for your family business.

- Create a budget and financial projections to ensure the financial sustainability of your family business.

- Outline the organizational structure and roles within the business to operate efficiently and harmoniously.

Small Town Politics, Broken Partnerships, And Financial Setback

Decades ago, in a small island town, I had aspirations of starting a new chapter and building a family business. Ever hopeful, I couldn't have been aware that I was also facing a multitude of challenges. With two small children to care for, I was eager to understand what steps I needed to take to get the ball rolling, but I lacked the experience, resources, and support that I needed to make my dreams a reality.

I didn't have much money, nor did I have any prior business or entrepreneurial experience. I struggled to understand how to keep books, secure small business financing, and who to consult to begin. At every turn, I faced obstacles that seemed insurmountable. I found myself caught in the middle of a series of frustrating and difficult situations, trying to navigate this new world of entrepreneurship while also being a single parent.

While I had escaped from the intense pressures of big city living to an island small town paradise, the beachfront property was confined to residential zoning restrictions. Business would not be allowed.

From the start, it was clear that a business location would have to be found. When a local company's mortgage was foreclosed, I saw an opportunity to negotiate a purchase for their property with the foreclosing bank. I made sure that I introduced myself to the owners of the business in foreclosure, to make sure they were aware of my plans, and ask them if they would have objections to my going forward. I felt empathy for their plight as I considered what a painful position they might be finding themselves in, having their property foreclosed and facing bankruptcy in their business.

They assured me they had no objections and wished me well in my pursuit of establishing a new business.

Once the bank had accepted my proposal and I was inspired by the possibility of this being a potential location, I set about a search for three other entrepreneurial-minded locals to either establish or relocate their businesses. The location was large enough to split four ways and if it was possible to secure a four-party partnership it would make the property purchase affordable for all concerned.

Luckily, I had been warned of the pitfalls of partnerships and so knew enough to proceed with caution. I wasn't about to make agreements with the bank before partner assurances were solid and payment secured. Partnerships can be problematic, and unfortunately, after weeks of creative problem-solving and planning, this plan fell apart. One of the partners didn't want to work with another.

We faced a resolvable problem and the remedy could have been simply to find another partner. Instead a nagging doubt stirred inside me, and ever one to listen to my gut instincts, I knew intuitively that this step was leading me in the wrong direction. At first blush, indeed this seemed like an ideal location, which well it might have been had I not been a mom to two small children, looking for a lifestyle design that would allow me more time with them. So, I opted out, informed the bank, and undeterred, sought out an alternative location that wouldn't involve partners.

As so often happens in life, this seeming misfortune turned magical when a friend approached me with an idea that made much lifestyle sense. Instead of a "one street downtown" shop which would have presented all kinds of obstacles to my dreams of an ideal lifestyle, child-minding problems being not the least, we entertained a forested property subdivide and rezone plan.

This time the collaboration seemed to speed forward, with intense planning on my part to make this project work for both my friend's family and mine, only to have the town planner refuse to greenlight the original development proposal. That formative agreement between two friends took many twists and turns. Multiple iterations later, before settling into something no one could have imagined out of its origin story, my friend settled elsewhere while I had a final location from which to start a new business. Little did I realize in the beginning that I would also get a 2.5 acre development project to last decades. But, I digress. Let's go back to the beginning.

More setbacks followed. Resilience ensued! To cite one example, the Ministry of Highways & Infrastructure initially approved my property development plan, only to change their mind and threaten to erect a concrete barrier that would severely limit customer access.

While gaining support from some quarters, I faced bureaucratic resistance from other officials in positions of power, including a member of the town council who took exception to my branding colors and tried to turn down my signage application. At every turn it seemed, I encountered opposition and challenges that tested my resolve and determination.

In addition to these external challenges, I struggled with my own limitations. I lacked organizational skills, consistency, and discipline. As an introvert, seeking out resources and meeting with various planning officials and regulators was daunting. The pressure of caring for two small children and trying to move forward with planning, the business weighed heavily on my shoulders. I felt overwhelmed and uncertain about the future.

Even when I set things in motion in meticulous order, everything seemed to fall apart. I ran into problems with planned business partners and had to figure out a lot of things on my own. I was forced to confront the reality that setbacks start at the beginning and will come continuously. I traversed a road full of unexpected surprises and financial setbacks, leaving me reeling from the challenges that seemed to multiply with each passing day.

Yet, in the midst of these trials, I discovered the power of resilience and the importance of seeking out allies. I learned to pivot and approach things from a different angle when my plans were challenged. I had to forego the idea of splitting a property and instead took on the entire property, learning how to subdivide and develop it by myself. This unexpected setback was a substantial blow, but I refused to give up on my dreams.

I sought out a retired government business advisor who became a mentor to me, guiding me through the complexities of small business planning and procedures. I also learned that setbacks are not the end of the road. "There is a reason for everything", my grandmother and her daughter, my mother, would say, even if it's rarely apparent in the moment. I found the courage to pivot and stay focused on the positive, no matter how difficult the circumstances became.

Through prayer and perseverance, I found the strength to face each new challenge with renewed determination. While I learned from a wise spiritual teacher that there are 99 ways to do the dishes, I applied the principle to my task at hand and determined that there are probably 99 ways to keep a set of books. During the test-phase days at the beach, when my children's father had also been interested in pursuing a family live/work lifestyle, he showed me several bookkeeping suggestions and I tried each until I settled on a system that I thought could work for me. Accounting and bookkeeping are not necessarily fed by any natural talents that I possess. Yet, I pushed on and learned to live with limitations. I soon discovered that interpreting reports and crafting projections are mission critical to developing systems in business. Today, it's easier for the beginner entrepreneur, who can pick from many accounting software choices.

From the beginning, I pushed through the setbacks and learned from each experience, ultimately emerging with a newfound sense of strength and resilience. I was grateful for the allies who believed in my vision and the community benefit that my business could bring. I became adept at knowing when to stand strong and fight, and when to pivot and approach things from a different angle. I accepted that the more people involved, the higher the likelihood of curve balls coming my way.

In the end, I learned that setbacks and challenges are an inherent part of the journey towards success. I became more resilient and adaptable, finding courage in the face of adversity. I was finally able to start my family business, and every obstacle along the way at the start-up stage only made me stronger and more determined. Through all the trials and tribulations, I had found the courage and love to push through and realize my dreams.

Now It's Time To Get Into Gear Planning Your Business, And Having Fun!

Congratulations on making it to this crucial step in building your family business! In this chapter, we will dive into the nitty-gritty of creating a business plan—a fundamental tool that will guide your business from vision to reality. Let's get started.

1: Identify The Target Market And Customer Demographics.

To create a successful business, you need to know who your customers are and what they need. Conduct thorough market research to identify your target market and understand their demographics, preferences, and behaviors. This will help you tailor your products or services to meet their specific needs, ultimately leading to more satisfied customers and increased sales.

For example, if your family business is a local bakery, you'll want to consider who your primary customer base will be—perhaps families looking for special occasion cakes, or local cafes in need of fresh bread and pastries.

Here Are Some Research Suggestions:

- Conduct surveys and analysis to understand the age, gender, income level, and education level of your target market.

- Utilize social media analytics to identify the geographic location and online behavior of your target customers.

- Gather data on lifestyle preferences, interests, and values of your potential customers to tailor your marketing messages.

- Review industry reports and studies to gain insights into the purchasing behavior and buying patterns of your target market.

- Study consumer trends and market trends to anticipate the needs and preferences of your target customers.

- Utilize customer feedback and testimonials to identify the pain points and desires of your target market.

- Create customer personas (called avatars) based on demographic information and psychographic details to better understand your target audience.

- Analyze data from previous sales to identify customer segments and who has been most responsive to your offerings. If there isn't any such data existent that would apply to your particular business idea, as was the case at the beginning of my business, then you have to *use your imagination and make it up! For more about that read on.*

- Consult with industry experts and consultants to gain insights into the demographic trends and customer behavior within your target market.

2: Develop A Marketing And Sales Strategy.

Once you know who your target market is, it's time to develop a marketing and sales strategy to reach them. This includes how you will promote your products or services, where you will sell them, and how you will attract and retain customers. Your strategy should be aligned with your target market's preferences and behaviors to ensure maximum effectiveness.

For instance, if your family business is an art supply store, your marketing strategy might include social media advertising, targeting artists and art students, as well as partnerships with local art schools and community arts organizations. Variations in your marketing strategies might be related to whether or not your art supply store is a virtual store or a bricks and mortar business.

First, begin by conducting market research to gain a better understanding of your target market's needs, preferences, and behaviors. You are aiming for your marketing and sales strategy to appeal directly to your target customer, so the better you can define who they are and how you can solve their problem, the more likely you are to have your marketing efforts land successfully. Who are they? And what do they want? Are they more likely to respond to social media marketing, traditional advertising, or word-of-mouth referrals? Understanding this will help you tailor your strategy to reach them in the most effective way.

Once you have a better understanding of your target market, it's time to create a compelling marketing message that speaks directly to them. This could include highlighting the benefits of your products or services, addressing their pain points, or showcasing how your business stands out from the competition. Be sure to communicate your message through all of your marketing channels, whether it's your website, social media, or in-person interactions.

Now that you have a strong marketing message, you'll need to determine the best channels to reach your targetted customer. This could include social media platforms, email marketing, or even participating in local community events. Consider where your target market spends their time and focus your efforts there. Remember, quality over quantity is key. It's better to have a strong presence in a few carefully chosen channels than to spread yourself too thin.

As you develop your sales strategy, consider the steps that customers will take from first hearing about your products or services to actually making a purchase. You might need 7 touchstones before the sale. Will they require a demonstration, a free trial, or a special offer? Learn how to create an effective sales funnel. Make the process as seamless and compelling as possible to encourage them to move through your sales funnel. An automated sales funnel is best. You would also do well to brainstorm various types of customer loyalty programs, and plan on implementing several in succession to test what works. Add on referral incentives and retain your customers' business long term.

You may also want to consider consultation with a master marketer. Sometimes, this can be a very costly route but can be well worth the investment, even if you are provided with only one excellently performing marketing message. You may be able to minimize your costs by purchasing one of their programs, courses or books for home study. Also, be on the lookout for guaranteed return on investment (ROI). Sometimes, a guarantee of a certain percentage increase in revenue as a result of employing the marketing tips offered, will allow you to focus your attention on what's working or not working and by how much the successful marketing tactics are impacting your bottom line. You may be offered a full refund of your purchase price if you are not able to triple your outlay for the program within a 6 month period, (as an example). This can be a phenomenal investment with huge payoff for the struggling beginner entrepreneur which could have profound long-term implications for the success of your business.

In conclusion, developing a marketing and sales strategy is crucial for the success of your business. By understanding your target market, crafting a compelling marketing message, choosing the right channels to reach them, and streamlining the sales process, you'll be well on your way to attracting and retaining customers. Remember to constantly evaluate and adjust your strategy as needed to stay ahead of the curve and continue growing your business.

3: Determine The Initial Investment And Funding Sources.

Every business requires some level of initial investment to get off the ground. Consider what you'll need to start and run your business, and explore potential funding sources such as personal savings, loans, grants, or investors. This is a crucial first step. Having a clear understanding of your initial investment needs and funding options will help you kick-start your family business with confidence.

Let's say your family business is a small organic farm. You'll need to consider the costs of land, equipment, and seeds, as well as ongoing expenses like labor and maintenance.

Whatever type of business you're considering it's going to be vital to take some time to sit down and really think about what you'll need to get your business off the ground. This might include start-up costs like purchasing equipment or inventory, as well as ongoing expenses like rent or mortgage costs, utilities, and payroll. Don't forget lifestyle needs for a would-be family business venture. If the children are very young, location might be mission-critical, as was the case when I first started, as you might remember from my search for a location for my family business in the story at the start of this chapter. Also, don't forget to factor in any marketing or advertising costs you might incur as you work to establish your brand and attract customers.

When it comes to funding your business, there are a variety of options to explore. Many entrepreneurs start by using their personal savings to fund their start-up costs. This can be a great option if you have a healthy amount of savings and are willing to take on some risk to get your business up and running. If you're not able to cover all of your initial investment needs with your personal funds, you might want to consider taking out a small business loan from a bank or other financial institution. Do you have friends or family members who can act as a funding source?

Another potential source of funding for your new business is grants. There are many government and private organizations that offer grants to help small businesses get off the ground. Though it can be competitive to secure a grant, it's definitely worth looking into as an option for funding your start-up costs. If you're open to giving up some ownership and control of your business, you might also consider seeking investors. These individuals or groups can provide the capital you need in exchange for a stake in your company.

Having a clear understanding of your initial investment needs and funding options will give you the confidence you need to move forward with your business plan. Utilize resources such as financial planning tools and business plan templates to help you organize your thoughts and put your ideas into action. Remember, many successful businesses started from humble beginnings, so don't be discouraged if you don't have a huge amount of funding to start with. With the right amount of determination and creativity, you can make your business dreams a reality!

4: Create A Budget And Financial Projections.

It's essential to create a detailed budget and financial projections to ensure the financial sustainability of your family business. This includes estimating your revenue, expenses, and cash flow, as well as projecting your business's financial performance over a specific period, such as one year or five years. This information will help you make informed decisions and demonstrate the potential profitability of your business to stakeholders.

Using a financial planning software like QuickBooks or FreshBooks can make the budgeting and projections process much smoother and more accurate.

A supremely important factor that might not be considered by most people embarking on their first entrepreneurial venture is money mindset. This is an essential aspect of any budding entrepreneur's journey and absolutely cannot be ignored. ***Pay attention to your money mindset.***

Perhaps you may even wonder what money mindset even means! If that's where you're at as you read this, make an intention to find out. If you're anything like me, born working-class British, understanding and getting a leg-up on evolving your money mindset can lead to a richly transformative experience in self-development and the ability to learn how to create and manage wealth.

Perhaps you were born into wealth but had no family financial guidance or formal financial education. This is quite possible as our educational system mostly leaves out money as part of the curriculum and for a lot of our history, money has been pretty much a taboo topic. You may have always taken money for granted and as a consequence have no idea how to manage it. If this resembles your situation, consider whether or not you think you've been set up for success. Then consider the possibility that you may have been set up for failure! Is it poverty mindset or prosperity mindset and how will you know? It can be a tough call to figure all this out on your own, as most of your mindset is pre-programmed, deeply embedded contents of the subconscious mind have you acting on autopilot, primarily set into being within your first 7 years of existence.

As We Consider Money Mindset, Let's Look At This Example:

You will probably either want, or be forced by a lending institution, to create a 1, 3, and 5 year business plan with low, medium, and high projections for each. I created a plan like that back in the day, before opening my doors for business. What happened years later was a surprise, when I stumbled upon those projections in my files, after I had forgotten all about them. The stark realization was that I had been spot on, *for all of the low projections*. There I had been, starting a business in a remote area, with a small local population whose tourist industry was at its earliest beginnings. I had zero precedents as a guide to use in creating those projections. In fact, I can give you an example of the ground breaking nature of this planned enterprise, as later on, when I borrowed a friend's old truck and drove to the border to pick up some imported surfboards from California, the Canadian border brokerage officials had no idea what import duty to charge me as they also had no precedent! *They asked ME what I thought the duty should be!* (They weren't having any of it when I suggested 0%) Again, I digress. Back to crafting a solid business plan and step-wise financial projections.

I had made up my projections from my imagination. It had been an exercise in imagining. Then I had to say to myself, "Imagine that! I made up all the numbers and I was spot on!" Why had it been precisely the low numbers, and not the high numbers that were so predictively accurate?

Interestingly, I knew enough about my own evolving money mindset by that time. I was able to recognize roots in a poverty mindset, knowing also that I was slowly evolving my conscious awareness and learning to embrace a prosperity mindset. I didn't yet know much about ambivalent motivations and neuroplastic reprogramming but I was learning and that incident proved quite the revelation - a terrific *stop and take notice* moment. I saw quite distinctly that I was dealing with something real and was on the right path to reprogramming. You see, it's not only the financial ramifications of this kind of bias that cramps one's style, and imposes limitations, but it's social as well. Just the same as placing limitations on the possibilities of expanding and experiencing abundance, a poverty mindset also imposes limitations on one's ability for expansiveness and positivity where wealth and wealthy people are in view. I hope my example stirs curiosity in you about your money mindset. I hope it helps you shine a light in the dark places and notice potential need to undo some of the early programming that has you running on autopilot instead of bringing conscious awareness to your thinking brain. Taking charge and shining a light of conscious awareness onto the contents of your *other than conscious* brain can guide you in a direction that frees you from bias and limitation, and helps you expand into an abundance mindset for your personal expansion, and for growing your family business.

I made a financial education an important aspect of our family business and gave both my kids a year-long investing challenge, beginning on their 13th birthday. This challenge game was both fun as an experience and pivotal in forming a future ability to create assets from a minimum wage position, rooted in practices from their earliest years. When it comes to money mindset transformation, it's key to remember that "you don't know what you don't know".

Another critical factor in building a successful business is having a tight grip on the bookkeeping. First, you must know how to read the books. There's no necessity for you to actually do the bookkeeping. It is certainly helpful, though not essential, for you to be involved in creating the initial general ledger for your books and having a thorough understanding of income and expenses, and be able to interpret an income statement, and a profit and loss statement. If you choose not to be involved in that aspect though, a word of warning. The reality is that the majority of business owners who experience bankruptcy for reasons other than business failure, experience it through not having this awareness and oversight, which makes them much more susceptible to embezzlement. It's actually not an uncommon route for many celebrities to take, frequently leading them to financial disaster. Sad but true!

5: Outline The Organizational Structure And Roles Within The Business.

Lastly, outline the organizational structure of your family business and define the roles and responsibilities of each family member or employee. Creating clear, well-defined roles will help your business operate efficiently and harmoniously, minimizing confusion and disputes. It will help you create a solid foundation for your family business to thrive.

First, let's look at the top of the hierarchy. This is probably the founder or CEO, who is responsible for setting the overall direction and strategy of the business. Initially, there may be only a CEO, or there may be several key roles such as the COO, CFO, and CMO, each responsible for specific functions within the company. These roles will vary depending on the nature of your business, but it's essential to have a clear understanding of who is in charge of what. Perhaps, in the beginning, these are the only top level labels you need to assign. However, you are going to require certain key positions called company directors, if you create a legal structure around your business. More on that later.

Next, let's delve into defining the roles and responsibilities of each family member or employee within the business. First, consider the strengths and weaknesses of each family member and assign roles that play to their strengths. For example, if one family member has a background in finance, they may be well-suited for the role of CFO. On the other hand, if another family member has a background in marketing, they may be best suited for the role of CMO. By assigning roles based on individual strengths and expertise, you can ensure that each family member is contributing to the success of the business.

In a completely different circumstance, such as starting a business when the children are small, children will slowly grow to help out, as their skills and schooling allow. It's prudent to rotate children through roles according to their age, as they take turns adding more responsible duties to their tasks, according to birth order sequence.

In addition to defining roles based on expertise or maturity, it's practical to consider the personalities and work styles of each family member. This can help prevent conflicts within the business and create more harmonious working relationships. For example, if one family member is more detail-oriented and organized, they may be well-suited for a role that involves managing operations and logistics. On the other hand, if another family member is more creative and visionary, they may be better suited for a role that involves developing innovative strategies for growth and expansion. Try to be flexible around these intentions. It's important. One of the great opportunities of having a family business is family creativity and collaboration. It's your family and your business and it should have a component of fun! There's no one else to impose hard and fast rules about organizational structure and you can suggest family members take on multiple responsibilities, emphasizing having the ability to morph and change. You may want to emphasize creative license to try new things, and to suggest ways for the business to evolve and pivot when necessary.

When assigning roles and responsibilities, it's also essential to establish clear lines of communication and decision-making processes. This will help prevent confusion and disputes within the business, ensuring that everyone knows who to report to, and how decisions will be made. Decide whether you are choosing hierarchy or a consensus model for the business.

Putting systems in place for resolving conflicts and disagreements can prove valuable, whether that involves regular family meetings, team-building exercises, or seeking outside mediation if necessary. If someone decides mediation is needed, how will you ensure mediation is brought in, if you don't have everyone bought into an agreement for mediation? Unless you decide in advance, there are no enforcers! Just a word of caution.

Will you want a hierarchy for employees of the family business or would you prefer a flat, less hierarchical structure. How will you implement a consensus model for employees if that is more aligned with your family values? Make a list of pros and cons to assist in these kinds of decisions.

Lastly, it's important to create a culture of transparency and open communication within the business. This will help foster trust and collaboration among family members and employees, creating a more positive and productive work environment. Clear expectations and goals for each role, and providing regular feedback and support, can help ensure that everyone is working towards the common goal of business success. You either have a bottom line and a profit model or you have a family hobby.

Remember, no one size fits all. Be creative. In conclusion, defining the organizational structure and roles within your family business is essential for creating a strong foundation for success. By considering the strengths, expertise, and personalities of each family member, assigning roles accordingly, and establishing clear lines of communication and decision-making processes, you can create a more efficient and harmonious work environment. Ultimately, this will help your family business thrive and grow for years to come.

Tools like Organimi for start-ups, Lucidchart or draw.io can help you visually map out your organizational structure, making it easier to communicate and understand. To bring it all together, you can find business plan templates from websites like SCORE(.org free template), Bplans, or LivePlan to guide you through the process and ensure you cover all the necessary components. You can also try AI Business Plan Generator. Don't forget to leverage market research tools such as Google Analytics or Facebook Insights to identify target demographics, and financial planning software to streamline your budgeting and projections.

Congratulations, you're well on your way to creating a solid business plan for your family business! In the next chapter, we will explore more essential steps as your business plan takes shape and helps you to form your business ideas into a more tangible and sustainable reality. Remember, this is the beginning of your journey to generational wealth, family creativity, lifestyle legacy, and financial freedom through your family business. Keep up the great work! And have Fun!

You Will Need:

- Business plan templates from websites like SCORE, Bplans, or LivePlan

- Market research tools to identify target demographics such as Google Analytics or Facebook Insights

- Financial planning software like QuickBooks or FreshBooks for budgeting and projections

- Organizational chart tools like Lucidchart or Microsoft Visio

Chapter Summary

➢ Identify the target market and customer demographics

➢ Develop a marketing and sales strategy

➢ Determine the initial investment and funding sources

➢ Create a budget and financial projections

➢ Outline the organizational structure and roles within the business

Chapter FAQ

Question: *What are the essential components of a business plan?*

Answer: The essential components of a business plan include a detailed description of the business, market analysis, marketing and sales strategies, organizational structure, financial projections, and funding requirements. These components are crucial for providing a comprehensive overview of your business and its potential for success.

Question: *How can I identify my target market and customer demographics?*

Answer: Conduct market research. This may involve using tools such as Google Analytics or Facebook Insights to gather data on the age groups, income levels, geographical locations, and preferences of your potential customers. Understanding this information will help tailor your products or services to meet their specific needs.

Question: *What are the different funding sources for a family business?*

Answer: Different funding sources for a family business may include personal savings, loans from financial institutions, investment from family and friends, venture capital, or angel investors. Each funding source has its pros and cons, and it's essential to carefully consider which option is most suitable for your business's financial needs.

Question: What are the best methods for creating financial projections?

Answer: Create a budget and forecast sales. The simplest and quickest is to make your own revenue template with monthly projections 1 year out then plot backwards weekly till today. All of my coaching clients are encouraged to do this reality grounding exercise for their first cash machine creation before giving up their 9-5. You can use financial planning software like QuickBooks or FreshBooks to help create a budget and forecast sales to project your future finances accurately. Consulting with a financial advisor or accountant can also provide valuable insight into creating realistic financial projections.

Question: How can I determine the roles and responsibilities within my family business?

Answer: Outline an organizational structure, defining the specific tasks and duties of each family member or employee. Clear communication and transparency are essential in establishing the roles within the business to ensure everyone understands their responsibilities.

Question: How can I estimate the initial investment needed to start my family business?

Answer: Calculate the costs of purchasing inventory, leasing a space, and hiring staff. Account for any other expenses such as marketing, website development, and legal fees. Consult with industry experts or experienced business owners in a similar field who can provide valuable insights into determining the initial investment requirements.

Question: What are some common mistakes to avoid when creating a business plan?

Answer: Some common mistakes to avoid when creating a business plan include vague or unrealistic financial projections, inadequate market research, lack of clarity in the business description, and neglecting to address potential risks and challenges. Thoroughly review and revise your business plan to ensure it is comprehensive, well-researched, and realistic.

Question: What are the benefits of having a comprehensive business plan for a family business?

Answer: The benefits of having a comprehensive business plan for a family business include providing a clear roadmap for success, attracting potential investors and partners, ensuring organized and strategic business operations, and serving as a tool for making informed business decisions. A well-thought-out business plan can assist in identifying potential challenges and opportunities within the business.

Legal Eagles And Financial Wizards: Establishing Your Family Business Backbone

This chapter will help you:

- Choose the appropriate legal structure for your family business, considering factors such as liability, taxes, and management.

- Understand the process and requirements for registering your business with the appropriate government authorities.

- Separate personal and business finances by opening a business bank account and obtaining necessary licenses and permits.

- Set up accounting and record-keeping systems using software such as Xero or Wave to ensure accurate financial records and compliance with tax obligations.

- Obtain business insurance to protect your family business against potential risks, such as property damage, liability, and business interruption.

The Disturbing Reality Of Copycatting: Don't Let Your Family Business Be Victimized

I never thought that a small decision could lead to such a big problem. You see, as the founder of a family business in a small island town a while back, things were going pretty well, but I knew we needed a new logo to help with our branding. That's when my good friend Jim, a talented tattoo artist, showed me one of his designs. I could see the potential in it, and I asked him if we could collaborate on redesigning it to use as the new shop logo. When reworked, the image was unique, bold, and held an air of creativity & lifestyle that perfectly encapsulated my vision for the family business. It was a beautiful and eye-catching image that really helped to elevate the business and make it stand out.

However, that's where the trouble began. You see, my friend had instructed me to put a copyright notification on the image with his signature underneath, to denote that he was legally entitled to ownership, known as copyright, as the creator of the image. If anyone were to use his image without his permission, they could be prosecuted. But the problem was that the image was inside a perfect circle, and his signature stuck out at the bottom, distorting the perfection of the circle. Despite this, we decided to move forward with it, not thinking it would be an issue.

We started using the logo on various products, from stickers to hoodies and t-shirts. It was clear from the beginning, the new logo was a hit. Customers loved it.

Little did I know, an order went out for new replacement stickers and other shop products with the beloved logo, but the submissions were made with the logo as a perfect circle, minus the copyright and artist signature at the bottom. I was completely unaware of this change, and the consequences of that oversight would soon become painfully clear.

One day, out of curiosity, my son and business partner was doing a Google search and discovered something shocking. His online search turned up a few shops in another country using our logo and brand. Someone had decided to copycat and we were able to view these shops online. Our shop had obviously been photographed and our branding replicated and items with our logo (including blatant location alteration) were on display everywhere inside.

We were shocked with the discovery. The violation was clear. Someone was copycatting, and staking claim to creative work that didn't belong to them and the initial sensation felt paralyzing, like there was nothing we could do about it.

That's when our family learned a valuable lesson. We realized that intellectual property theft is rampant, and sometimes you cannot afford to not have legal protection. It was a tough lesson to learn, but it was a wake-up call for the three of us: myself and my son and daughter, who are my two business partners. We knew we needed to take action, so my son reached out to a personal contact who helped us find a lawyer in the offending country. With their help, we were able to get compliance and force the copycat to stop using our logo and branding.

The experience was a harsh reminder that sometimes, overlooking the little details can lead to big consequences. From that day forward, we would do our best to protect our intellectual property and have the foresight to pay attention to the legal security of our creations. Of course, that's a tall order, but experiences like this help create resilience and durability, especially where our business interests are concerned. It was a hard-learned lesson, but it was a necessary one. I hope our story serves as a cautionary tale to others - do your utmost to protect what's yours, or someone else might try to take advantage of you.

While this was not the only experience we've endured over the years where we have been legally challenged in business, we can hope that our past challenges make us a little more eagle-eyed. Unfortunately, lawsuits are rampant today, so if you happen to live in Japan or the U.S., double down on your take-aways from this lesson, as the litigation statistics in both countries are through the roof. Furthermore, 10 year-old statistics tell us that there are 16,000 judges in Brazil and more lawyers per capita than in the U.S.

As your family business grows, a useful principle to follow is get the best accounting and legal help that your business can afford. Now it's your turn to *get ready to lawyer up* as you prepare to embark on your family business adventure! This might be an odd place to repeat it but don't forget to have Fun! And congratulations on coming this far in your journey to start a family business! Now that you have your business idea and plan in place, it's time to establish a solid legal and financial foundation for your new venture. In this chapter, we'll walk you through the key steps to help ensure that your family business is legally and financially sound.

1: Choose The Legal Structure For The Business.

The first step in establishing a solid legal foundation for your family business is to choose the right legal structure. There will usually be several options to consider, depending on where you are establishing your business. Each structure has its own advantages and disadvantages in terms of liability, taxes, and management. It's important to carefully consider which structure aligns best with your business goals and consult with a legal professional for guidance.

When starting your own business, one of the most important decisions you'll make is choosing the legal structure for your venture. The legal structure you choose will have a significant impact on how your business operates, how it is taxed, and how it is protected from potential liabilities. It's essential to carefully weigh the pros and cons of each option and choose the structure that best aligns with your long-term goals.

Where I live we have two primary options. We can legally incorporate.

A corporation is a separate legal entity that can shield its owners from personal liability and has the ability to raise capital through the sale of stock. However, corporations are also subject to double taxation, meaning that profits are taxed at the corporate level and then again at the individual level when distributed to shareholders. While this structure offers strong liability protection, it can be more complex and expensive to establish and maintain.

If we don't choose to incorporate another option is to register a DBA name. This is known as assuming a trade name and the purpose is to alert the public that you are conducting business under a name other than your personal legal name. Depending on the county, state, province or country where your business is established, these legal structures will vary and you will have to familiarize yourself with your legal structure options according to the territory where your company is going to be established.

If you are establishing a U.S. business, your corresponding options to the ones cited above would be a corporation or an LLC. An LLC offers the limited liability of a corporation, meaning that the owners' personal assets are protected in the event of a lawsuit or debt. It also offers the flexibility of a partnership, allowing for the pass-through taxation of profits and losses. This can be a great option for small businesses looking for protection and flexibility.

For those looking to start a business with someone else, a partnership may be the best option. A general partnership offers flexibility and simplicity, but also comes with the potential for personal liability for the debts and obligations of the business. Limited partnerships, on the other hand, allow some partners to have limited liability while others have full liability. Partnerships are often a good choice for businesses with multiple owners who want to share control and decision-making.

It's important to consider not only the immediate needs of your business, but also its long-term goals. How do you envision your business growing? Do you plan to seek outside investment or take your company public? These are important questions to consider when choosing a legal structure. Additionally, consulting with a legal professional can provide you with valuable insight and guidance as you make this critical decision.

As you weigh your options and consider the potential impact of each legal structure, remember that there is no one-size-fits-all solution. Each business is unique, with its own set of circumstances and goals. Take the time to carefully evaluate your choices and seek out the support and advice you need to make an informed decision.

As you seek professional advice, realize that no one else can make decisions for you. In the early years of my business, my research led me to a decision that it would be a wise choice to incorporate. I sought advice from accountants and lawyers and the general advice that came back was not to incorporate. I chose to put off the decision to incorporate for years and experienced too much anxiety in delaying the inevitable. The professionals from whom I sought advice were good, honest people with integrity and my best intentions at heart. I felt that their experience led them to choices that were best for them and different from what I needed. In the end, the incorporation was time consuming but relatively straightforward and the relief it provided when finally done, was enormous.

Your business will be the result of your hard work, passion, and vision. Protecting it through the right legal structure is an essential step in ensuring its long-term success. With the right foundation in place, you can confidently move forward and focus on what you do best – building and growing your business.

2: Register The Business With The Appropriate Government Authorities.

Once you have chosen the legal structure for your family business, you'll need to register it with the appropriate government authorities. This typically involves filing the necessary paperwork and paying the required fees. The process varies depending on your chosen legal structure and your location, so do your research about specific requirements in your area.

3: Open A Business Bank Account And Obtain Necessary Licenses And Permits.

When it comes to setting up your family business, one of the first steps you'll want to take is to open a business bank account. Opening a business bank account provides a clear distinction between your personal assets and those of the business. This is crucial for maintaining the legal and financial integrity of your venture. Separating your personal and business finances, goes a long way to help ensure that your company's funds are properly accounted for and that your personal assets are protected.

To open a business bank account, you'll typically need to provide various documents, including your business license or registration, articles of incorporation, and a partnership agreement if you have partners. It will be beneficial to shop around and compare different business accounts to find the one that best suits the operational, budgetary and regulatory needs of your family business.

Once you have your business bank account set up, it's time to move on to obtaining any necessary licenses and permits for your industry and location. This could include more than just your business license.

Additionally you may need a sales tax permit, health department permit, or professional license if you are operating in a regulated industry such as healthcare or finance. These are all essential for ensuring that you are compliant with local regulations and able to operate legally.

While the process of obtaining licenses and permits may seem daunting, it's important to stay organized and work through the requirements step by step. Reach out to your local government or industry associations for guidance and support in navigating the process. Remember, these licenses and permits are not just legal requirements – they also demonstrate to your customers and partners that you are a credible and trustworthy business.

Once you have all your necessary licenses and permits in place, it's important to keep track of their expiration dates and any renewal requirements. Stay on top of these deadlines to ensure that your business remains in good standing and doesn't face any disruptions in its operations. It's a good idea to maintain an end of year checklist that accompanies your checklist for annual income tax preparation such as you might be given by your accountant. This will help ensure that you don't miss any of these important expiration dates that could put your family business out of business.

As you go through the process of opening a business bank account and obtaining licenses and permits, remember that this is all part of building a strong foundation for your family business. By taking the time to set up these essential financial and legal structures, you are creating a solid framework for your company to grow and thrive. Ideally, all family members involved in the family business need to be aware of the importance of these regulatory requirements and how to maintain your family business's compliance.

And finally, don't be afraid to seek help and advice from others who have gone through this process. There are many resources available to entrepreneurs, including business advisors, mentorship programs, and online forums where you can connect with fellow business owners. By learning from the experiences of others, you can gain valuable insights and avoid common pitfalls as you embark on this exciting journey.

In conclusion, opening a business bank account and obtaining necessary licenses and permits are crucial steps in ensuring the legal and financial integrity of your family business. By staying organized, seeking guidance when needed, and keeping a focus on compliance, you are setting the stage for your business to succeed and thrive for years to come.

4: Set Up Accounting And Record-Keeping Systems.

Accurate financial records and record-keeping systems are crucial for managing your family business's finances, complying with tax obligations and ensuring the success and growth of your venture. By maintaining accurate financial records, and assiduously maintaining other accurate record-keeping systems you will not only be able to manage your business's finances effectively, but these will assist you in complying with tax obligations, making informed decisions and accessing funding now and in the future. All these work together to propel your business forward.

When it comes to setting up your accounting and record-keeping systems, it is important to consider using accounting software to streamline the process. There are various options available, such as Quickbooks, Sage, Xero, or Wave, which are designed to help small businesses manage their finances with ease. These software programs can help you track your business's income and expenses, generate financial reports, and even manage payroll if you have employees.

Again, as in setting up legal structures for your business, it will be important to consider your location as you determine not only which software will work for where you do business, but also to consider the specific needs your business has with regard to what your bookkeeping and accounting systems will provide. For example, if you want to bring in a virtual assistant to keep your business books, then you would need to consider what systems the company or individual you plan to work with will need you to have, in order for them to agree to work with you.

By using accounting software, you can simplify the task of record-keeping and ensure that your financial records are organized and up to date. This will not only save you time and effort, but also provide you with a clear picture of your business's financial health, which is essential for making informed decisions.

Multiple factors directly relating to the needs of the business you're creating, may come into play when making a choice of available accounting software. Some software programs provide limited capacity and you might find yourself needing to use multiple systems. Some have fully integrated modules and can appear prohibitively expensive for a new business. However, it's important to future think. What are your big goals for the future of your business?

Trying to make the switch midstream to a new product because of the growing demands of your business when these systems have become part of the backbone of your operations, can wreak havoc on your day to day operations as you try to meet the demands of expansion. Will you have employees? Do you need a payroll module? Will you have products to sell? Will you have a handful, hundreds, thousands, or hundreds of thousands of products? What capacity will your inventory module need to deliver? Is you business bricks and mortar, online, or a combination of both? Do you need to have an online store? Will you have the need to segment your General Ledger? Will you need a software program that you can use for multiple businesses? These, and many other questions that you can consider in the early days will serve you well as you imagine the ideal future of your family business. All involved family members should familiarize themselves with these necessary systems and prepare to become competent in operations oversight.

In addition to helping you manage your finances efficiently, keeping organized financial records will be essential and beneficial for accessing funding in the future. Whether you are looking to apply for a business loan or seek investment from potential partners, having accurate and comprehensive financial records will build trust and credibility with lenders and investors.

As you embark on the journey of setting up your accounting and record-keeping systems, you must approach this task with a sense of organization and discipline.

Dedicate specific time each week to manage your finances, input transactions, and reconcile accounts. By making it a regular habit, you can stay on top of your business's financial activities and ensure that your records are always up to date.

Furthermore, consider seeking professional help if you are not confident in managing your accounting and record-keeping systems on your own. Hiring an accountant or bookkeeper can provide you with expert guidance and ensure that your financial records are maintained accurately. They can also help you navigate through tax obligations, maintain compliance with regulations, and provide valuable insights into your business's financial performance.

In conclusion, setting up accounting and record-keeping systems is essential for the success and growth of your family business. By using accounting software, maintaining organized financial records, and seeking professional help when needed, you can ensure that your business's finances are managed effectively and that you are well-prepared for future opportunities and challenges. So, take the time to set up your accounting and record-keeping systems with diligence and care, and watch and stay vigilant as your family business thrives.

5: Purchase Business Insurance To Protect Against Potential Risks.

Lastly, it's important to safeguard your family business against potential risks by obtaining business insurance. This can include coverage for property damage, liability, and business interruption. Investing in adequate insurance coverage provides peace of mind and protects your business from unforeseen circumstances.

By following these key steps, you can establish a solid legal and financial foundation for your family business, setting it up for long-term success and growth. Remember that the resources available such as LegalZoom, government websites, and accounting software, will be location dependent and can provide valuable guidance and support as you navigate this process. With the right legal and financial framework in place, you'll be well-equipped to focus on the creative and operational aspects of your family business, knowing that its foundation is secure. Best of luck on your entrepreneurial journey!

Chapter Summary

> ➢ Choose the legal structure for the business

> ➢ Register the business with the appropriate government authorities

> ➢ Open a business bank account and obtain necessary licenses and permits

> ➢ Set up accounting and record-keeping systems

> ➢ Purchase business insurance to protect against potential risks

Chapter FAQ

Question: *What are the specific requirements for registering a family business with government authorities?*

Answer: The specific requirements for registering a family business with government authorities depend on the chosen legal structure and location. Generally, it involves filing necessary paperwork and paying required fees. For example, the process for establishing a DBA in Canada or registering an LLC in the U.S., may differ from registering a corporation, and the requirements may vary from province or province or state to state, or will depend on the country in which the business is founded.

Question: *How can a family business protect personal assets from business liabilities when choosing a legal structure?*

Answer: A family business can protect personal assets from business liabilities by choosing the appropriate legal structure for their location.

Question: *What are the necessary licenses and permits that a family business might need to obtain?*

Answer: The necessary licenses and permits for a family business depend on the industry and location. Examples of licenses and permits include business operation licenses, health permits, zoning permits, and professional licenses.

Researching the specific requirements in your area and industry is crucial to ensure compliance with regulations.

Question: How can diversification of the family business help minimize risks?

Answer: Diversifying the family business across different sectors or markets can help minimize risks by spreading investments and revenue streams. For example, if one sector experiences a downturn, the family business can rely on the revenues from other diversified sectors to mitigate the impact. This helps in creating a more stable and resilient business in the long run.

Question: What benefits can be derived from reinvesting profits back into the family business?

Answer: Reinvesting profits back into the family business can fund expansion initiatives, hiring new talent, or investing in technology to stay competitive in the market. It also allows for sustainable growth and can help in diversifying the business across different sectors or markets, minimizing risks and creating a more stable and resilient business for the long haul.

The Art Of Selling: Driving Revenue For Your Family Business

This chapter will help you:

- Understand the importance of targeted advertising campaigns on social media and other platforms to reach potential customers and drive sales.

- Learn how to network and build strategic partnerships within the industry to expand your customer base and enhance your business's credibility and reputation.

- Implement promotions and loyalty programs to attract and retain customers, cultivate long-term relationships and encourage repeat business.

- Empower your family members to be effective salespeople through training and resources, ensuring alignment with the same sales strategies and goals.

- Measure and analyze the success of marketing efforts to continuously improve, making data-driven decisions to optimize your marketing strategies and drive revenue for your family business.

From Scarcity To Abundance: Raising Financially Savvy Children In Your Family Business

As a single mom and a founder of a budding family business, I knew I had a responsibility to set a positive example for my two young children. My goal was to provide them with a financial education that they wouldn't receive in school and to instill in them a positivity and prosperity mindset. However, I was faced with a significant obstacle - my own self-identity as a working-class immigrant. As I learned more about my own inner programming I began to acknowledge that I had a fair number of personal development lessons in front of me on this journey of transformation from poverty to prosperity mindset.

I was on a personal mission to transform my own perceived poverty mindset into a prosperity mindset and vitally aware that it takes time to reset those deeply rutted pathways of negative self-talk and ambivalent motivations. I obviously had not reached a full transformation while my kids were still very young and I was still experiencing myself struggling financially. Therefore, I had concluded that I might not be the ideal model for the mindset I wished to model for my children. I was concerned that I might unwittingly pass on a poverty mindset, when what I truly wanted was to teach them about abundance and wealth creation.

I realized that in order to truly teach my children about prosperity, I needed to continue working on transforming the limitations of my own programming. As I delved into the process of reprogramming my thoughts, language and beliefs about money, I also started teaching my children about the value of saving and investing. During their summer breaks from school, I encouraged them to work at the family business and put the bulk of their earnings into a GIC (Guaranteed Investment Certificate) for saving for a down payment on a future home, when they became of age. I wanted them to understand the concept of accumulating assets and the value of property, while also fostering an entrepreneurial spirit within them.

Yet, as I guided my children through these financial lessons, I wasn't sure if I had completely transformed my own mindset to exemplify a full abundance outlook. The family business was still in its early stages. It had passed the crucial five year mark, was still operational, so statistically doing better than most new businesses - the majority of which would have gone into bankruptcy by now, however we continued to face financial challenges. Despite this, I knew that it was crucial for the success of our business that we all have a prosperity mindset, and that we understand the principles of having money work for us.

So, I decided to implement a year-long challenge for both my son and my daughter when they each reached their 13th birthday. With the support of their grandmother, she agreed to participate with the kids in a year long experiment that I proposed. Their grannie, my mom, prided herself on being an astute investor. She is sharp and savvy, and continues to invest in her senior years. She'll be celebrating her 95th birthday this year! Grannie was game for the challenge with her grandkids. At their 13th birthday both the birthday boy (or girl) and she, began with a small amount of cash to start them off on this experiment, and each had a small monthly increment to add to their investments. During their year, I provided each of my kids with guidance on different types of investments, and the challenge was to see who could make the most money by the end of the year--Grannie or her 13 year old grandchild.

In addition to this challenge, from their earliest years through adolesence, I gave them each a very small weekly allowance that was provided freely and not transactionally linked to household chores. As an aside though, because they were growing up in a 3 person household they were always expected to contribute their part in household chores. I taught them the importance of dividing their allowance into three buckets - for immediate expenses, for medium-term expenses, and for long-range goals, with equal allocations in each. This allowed them to understand the principles of saving and investing, and the impact of their money mindset on our family business's financial success. From a very early age they both seemed to enjoy participating in the family business, and were encouraged to be creative about how they wanted to contribute. Little did I know at the time, the extent to which their leadership, business acumen and accomplishments would eventually far surpass mine.

As their investing challenge year progressed, each teen learned valuable lessons about saving and investing. They began to comprehend that their mindset towards money and abundance in all its forms, directly impacted their personal potential and our family business's potential for financial success. They also learned how to make money work for them, alongside their participation in the family business, which taught them the value of working for money.

Through this experience, they gained insight into their own comfort levels with risk and security, and developed a deeper understanding of financial principles. This transformative journey not only benefited them as individuals but also had a positive impact on our family business, as they became more involved and proactive in its growth.

In the end, this challenge not only taught my children about financial literacy and wealth creation but it also allowed me to witness their growth and development firsthand. Their passion for entrepreneurship ignited, and they emerged from this experience with a newfound sense of responsibility and a deeper appreciation for the value of money.

As a family, we had overcome the obstacle of a poverty mindset and had embraced a new perspective on wealth creation, all while strengthening the foundation of our family business. Through this journey, we had not only laid the groundwork for a successful family business but had also fostered a legacy of financial empowerment and abundance for generations to come. It was a journey of growth, resilience, and triumph, and it left us all feeling inspired and motivated to continue pursuing our dreams with unwavering determination.

Now we'll look at what it means to focus on the bottom line in your family business.

In this chapter, we will explore the essential strategies for implementing effective marketing and sales techniques to drive revenue for your family business. Whether you're selling a product or service, mastering the art of selling is crucial for the success of your business.

1: Launch Targeted Advertising Campaigns On Social Media And Other Platforms.

As a beginner entrepreneur, one of the most important steps in growing your business is to launch targeted advertising campaigns on social media and other platforms. This is a great way to reach potential customers and increase brand awareness. By targeting specific audiences, you can ensure that your advertising efforts are reaching the right people and getting the best possible results. The topic of branding is broad and it's not going to be included in this blueprint for setting up your family business. As you take forward steps in marketing continuing to place importance on your business branding will serve you well. Remember these go hand in hand.

The first step in launching targeted advertising campaigns is to identify your target audience. Who are the people that are most likely to be interested in your products or services? What are their demographics, interests, and behaviors? Once you have a clear understanding of your target audience, you can begin to create advertising campaigns that are tailored to their specific needs and preferences.

When creating your advertising campaigns, it's important to choose the right platforms to reach your target audience. Social media platforms like Meta, Instagram, Threads and X are great for reaching a wide audience, while platforms like LinkedIn are better for targeting business professionals. You may also need to advertise locally using hard-copy brochures, signage, etc. Consider the unique characteristics of each platform and how each aligns with your target audience's preferences.

To reach potential customers, you need to be present where they spend their time. Social media platforms provide powerful advertising tools that allow you to target specific demographics, interests, and behaviors. With platforms like Facebook Ads Manager or Google Ads, you can create tailored campaigns to reach your ideal customers and drive sales.

For example, if you're selling handmade jewelry for young adults, you can create a targeted advertising campaign on Instagram to reach users in the 18-30 age range who are interested in fashion and accessories.

Once you've chosen your platforms, it's time to create compelling ad content. The key to successful advertising campaigns is to create content that speaks directly to your target audience. Use language, imagery, and messaging that resonates with them and addresses their pain points or desires. The more personalized and targeted your content is, the more likely it is to capture the attention of your audience. An awareness of the significance of intergenerational distinctions hopefully will be a given in your successful family business. So you may already have an advantage when it comes to targeting a multi-generational market in your various advertising campaigns.

When launching your advertising campaigns, remember to set clear goals and objectives. What do you hope to achieve with your campaigns? Are you looking to increase website traffic, generate leads, or drive sales? By setting specific and clear goals, you can measure the success of your campaigns and make adjustments as needed.

Monitor performance closely as you launch your campaigns. This is important and not to be ignored. How will you tell if your marketing is working if you're not assessing their performance and impact on your bottom line. If your not creating effective advertising you're throwing money away. Pay attention to key metrics like click-through rates, engagement, and conversions. This will help you understand what's working and what's not, and allow you to make data-driven decisions to optimize your campaigns for better results.

In addition to monitoring performance, it's important to continuously test and refine your advertising campaigns. Try different ad formats, messaging, and targeting options to see what resonates best with your current audience, as this audience will have a tendency to morph and change over time, and as your business grows. By testing and refining your campaigns, you can improve their effectiveness and maximize your return on investment.

Finally, don't be afraid to seek help or advice when launching targeted campaigns. There are plenty of resources and experts available to help you navigate the world of digital advertising. Whether it's consulting with a marketing agency, taking an online course, or seeking mentorship from experienced entrepreneurs, there are plenty of ways to gain the knowledge and support you need to launch successful advertising campaigns. Remember, reaching out for help is a sign of strength, not weakness.

In conclusion, launching targeted advertising campaigns on social media and other platforms is an essential step in growing your business. By identifying your target audience, choosing the right platforms, creating compelling ad content, setting clear goals, monitoring performance, testing and refining, and seeking help when needed, you can create effective advertising campaigns that drive results. With the right approach and mindset, you can reach and engage your target audience, and ultimately, grow your business. So go ahead and launch those campaigns - the world is waiting to see what you have to offer!

2: Network And Build Strategic Partnerships Within The Industry.

In today's competitive industry environment, networking and building strategic partnerships are essential for business growth and success. By expanding your professional network and forming partnerships with other businesses, you can open doors to new opportunities and collaborations, reaching new customers, increasing your credibility, and elevating your business to new heights. Building strategic partnerships boosts your reputation and expands your visibility.

For instance, if you're running a family-owned bakery, you can partner with a local coffee shop to offer your products in their store, reaching a wider audience and increasing sales.

In this examples list, we will explore various ways in which effective networking and partnerships can benefit your business and provide real-world examples of successful collaborations within the industry:

- **Attend industry events and conferences**

Attending industry events and conferences allows you to connect with potential partners and customers face-to-face, providing a valuable opportunity to build lasting relationships.

- **Join industry-specific networking groups**

Joining networking groups specific to your industry

allows you to connect with like-minded professionals who can offer valuable insights and potential partnerships.

- **Utilize social media platforms**

Leveraging social media platforms such as LinkedIn and X can help you connect with industry professionals and potential customers on a global scale.

- **Collaborate on industry-specific projects**

Collaborating with other businesses on industry-specific projects can help you access new markets and build strategic partnerships.

- **Offer to speak at industry events**

Speaking at industry events can position you as an expert in your field and help you forge valuable connections with potential partners and customers.

- **Provide value to your connections**

Offering valuable resources, insights, or introductions to your network can help solidify your reputation as a trusted and valuable partner in the industry.

- **Host industry networking events**

Hosting your own industry networking events can help you establish yourself as a leader in the field and connect with potential partners and customers in a meaningful way.

- **Create a referral program**

Establishing a referral program can incentivize current customers and partners to refer new business to you, helping to expand your customer base.

- **Establish strategic partnerships with complementary businesses**

Forming partnerships with businesses that offer complementary services or products can help you provide additional value to your customers and expand your reach.

- **Leverage industry influencers**

Connecting with industry influencers can help you expand your reach and credibility within the industry, leading to new partnerships and customers.

- **Continuously nurture and maintain relationships**

Building and maintaining relationships is an ongoing process. Continuously nurturing and maintaining your connections can lead to lasting partnerships and a strong industry reputation.

3: Offer Promotions And Loyalty Programs To Attract And Retain Customers.

Creating promotions and loyalty programs is an effective way to incentivize customers to make a purchase and keep them coming back for more. Whether it's offering a discount on their first purchase or implementing a points-based loyalty program, these initiatives can help cultivate long-term relationships with your customers.

For example, a loyalty program can reward customers with points for every purchase, which they can then redeem for discounts or free products, encouraging repeat business and customer retention.

4: Train And Empower Family Members To Be Effective Salespeople.

Empower your family members to become effective salespeople by providing them with the necessary training and resources. Sales training resources such as books, online courses, or sales coaches can help them hone their skills and become confident communicators. Building a strong sales team within your family business will ensure that everyone is aligned with the same sales strategies and goals. For instance, conducting role-playing exercises as part of the training process can help family members practice their sales pitches and improve their persuasive abilities.

Be an example to your children as they grow up in the family business. Model constant and never ending improvement (CANI) to them as you exemplify this. Share your own personal development training resources with them. Keep the lines of communication open so that you pay attention to how interested they are in the topics you are sharing and talk with them openly and flexibly so that you are showing not telling.

It's important to realize that your family members may not inherently possess the skills and confidence needed to excel in sales. But with the right training and resources, they can unlock their potential and become highly effective salespeople. By investing in their development, you are not only helping them grow as individuals but also contributing to the success of your business. Try to allow room for individual personality traits to guide their interests and involvement in selling for the business, rather than steering them in directions that might have them feeling forced rather than inspired.

Start by providing your family members with access to sales training resources. This could include books on sales techniques, online courses, or even hiring a sales coach to work with them directly. Make it a point to discuss and share these resources with them, and encourage them to take advantage of these opportunities for growth.

It's also important to lead by example. Show your family members what effective salesmanship looks like by demonstrating it yourself. Take the time to teach them about the strategies and approaches that have worked for you in the past, and share your insights and experiences with them. This will help them learn from your expertise and build their confidence in their own abilities.

Encourage them as their talents and expertise start to develop and show. Utilize open communication and feedback. Create an environment where your family members feel comfortable sharing their thoughts, ideas, and concerns about their sales efforts. By being open to their input, you can help them overcome any hurdles they may be facing and provide them with the support they need to succeed. You also encourage their leadership in areas where they stand out and shine!

Set clear goals and expectations for your family members. Discuss the targets and benchmarks you have in mind for sales performance, and provide them with the tools and resources they need to reach these goals. By establishing clear expectations, you can motivate them to strive for excellence and hold themselves accountable for their results. This approach is important as you guide your children to be leaders in the family business. They will need access to the targets and benchmarks so they, in turn, can help lead the team forward. Your example should always set them up to be effective leaders who in turn, embrace the confidence to encourage others to lead.

It's important to foster a sense of teamwork and collaboration among your family members. Encourage them to work together, support each other, and share best practices. By creating a collaborative environment, you can leverage the strengths of each family member and harness the power of a united sales team.

Celebrate their successes and recognize their achievements. Acknowledge the hard work and dedication your family members put into their sales efforts, and show your appreciation for their contributions. Whether it's a simple pat on the back or a public recognition, let them know that their efforts are valued and that you are proud of their accomplishments.

Keep an open mind and be willing to adapt your sales strategies based on the feedback and input of your family members. Embrace their fresh perspectives and innovative ideas, and be open to trying new approaches that may improve your sales performance. By fostering a culture of innovation, you can stimulate continuous growth and development within your sales team.

Provide ongoing support and mentorship to your family members. Be available to assist them with any challenges they may face, and offer them guidance and advice to help them navigate through their sales responsibilities. By serving as a mentor, you can help them develop their skills and overcome obstacles that may be hindering their progress.

Lastly, remember to be patient and understanding as your family members grow into their roles as salespeople. It takes time and practice for them to refine their skills and become proficient in sales. Be supportive of their journey and offer them the encouragement they need to keep pushing forward.

By training and empowering your family members to become effective salespeople, you are not only strengthening your family business, but also laying the foundation for their personal and professional growth. With the right resources, guidance, and support, your family members can become confident, accomplished salespeople who contribute to, and ultimately lead the success of your business.

5: Measure And Analyze The Success Of Marketing Efforts To Continuously Improve.

To ensure the effectiveness of your marketing strategies, it's crucial to measure and analyze the results. Tools like Google Analytics or Kissmetrics can provide valuable insights into the performance of your marketing campaigns, website traffic, and customer behavior. By tracking key metrics such as conversion rates, customer acquisition cost, and customer lifetime value, you can make data-driven decisions to optimize your marketing efforts.

For instance, by analyzing the data from a recent email marketing campaign, you may discover that customers who received a certain promotional offer had a higher conversion rate, prompting you to replicate that offer in future campaigns.

Resources:

To aid you in implementing these strategies, you can utilize various tools and resources:

- Social media advertising platforms such as Facebook Ads Manager or Google Ads

- Networking events and industry conferences for building partnerships

- Loyalty program software like Smile.io or Yotpo

- Sales training resources such as books, online courses, or sales coaches

- Analytics tools like Google Analytics or Kissmetrics for measuring marketing success

By implementing these effective marketing and sales strategies, you can drive revenue for your family business, attract and retain customers, and ultimately achieve your business goals. Remember, continuous improvement and adaptability are key to staying ahead in the competitive marketplace.

Chapter Summary

➢ Launch targeted advertising campaigns on social media and other platforms

➢ Network and build strategic partnerships within the industry

➢ Offer promotions and loyalty programs to attract and retain customers

➢ Train and empower family members to be effective salespeople

➢ Measure and analyze the success of marketing efforts to continuously improve

Chapter FAQ

Question: *What are the key steps in implementing effective marketing and sales strategies to drive revenue for my family business?*

Answer: The key steps in implementing effective marketing and sales strategies include launching targeted advertising campaigns, networking and building strategic partnerships, offering promotions and loyalty programs, training and empowering family members as salespeople, and measuring and analyzing the success of marketing efforts for continuous improvement.

Question: *How can I ensure that my family business stays ahead in the competitive marketplace?*

Answer: To ensure that your family business stays ahead in the competitive marketplace, continuous improvement and adaptability are key. By constantly refining your marketing and sales strategies based on data-driven decisions and staying updated with industry trends, you can maintain a competitive edge in the marketplace.

Question: *Why is it important to continuously measure and analyze the success of marketing efforts?*

Answer: It is important to continuously measure and analyze the success of marketing efforts to make data-driven decisions and optimize your strategies. By tracking key metrics such as conversion rates, customer acquisition cost, and customer lifetime value, you can gain valuable insights that allow you to refine and improve your marketing and sales tactics, leading to increased revenue and customer retention.

Creating A Culture of Empowerment and Collaboration

This chapter will help you:

- Cultivate a positive company culture and team dynamics that promote trust, respect, and open communication

- Establish clear communication channels and regular family business meetings to streamline internal communication and maintain transparency

- Foster a supportive and collaborative work environment that emphasizes teamwork, idea-sharing, and recognizing the unique strengths of each team member

- Provide ongoing training and professional development opportunities to invest in the growth and development of your team

- Recognize and reward individual and team achievements to foster a sense of appreciation and motivation within the team and address and resolve conflicts promptly through open dialogue

From Toddlers To Top Leaders: How This Family Business Transformed Through The Generations

As the founder of a family business in a small town, I never anticipated the journey that lay ahead for me and my two young children. However, the moment I opened the doors of that first tiny shop, even though my children were only small, I knew that it was going to be the perfect opportunity for our family to come together and create something special. With my two young children by my side, it was a dream come true, and I imagined seeing them grow up in the business, learning and evolving into leaders.

After several years of business and a couple of iterations, our slightly larger, but still small shop began to gain traction. My children, who were then in their early teen years, naturally started assuming more leadership roles within the business. Their passion for the entrepreneurial aspect of our family business was palpable, and I was determined to support their aspirations and creative engagement in every way possible.

However, as they began to take on more responsibilities, a conflict arose within the business. Some of the other handful of employees, who were locals of our small tourist town, started to feel as though my children were receiving preferential treatment due to their familial connection to the business. They were concerned that my children's emergence in leadership roles would potentially put them at a disadvantage within the company.

As I became aware of some of this dynamic, I worried that the social pressure and envy from older employees might make it difficult for my kids to thrive as they grew into leadership roles. I wanted to ensure that my children were supported, but I also recognized the value that each employee brought to the business. It was a delicate balance, and I was determined to find a solution that honored both the aspirations of my children and the contributions of the other employees.

The conflict came to a head when one of the employees, unable to accept the inevitable shift in leadership dynamics, decided to quit and open her own shop, thereby becoming a direct competitor. It was a challenging and disheartening time for our family business, but it also presented an opportunity for growth and realization.

Through this experience, I learned that the evolution of leadership within a family business is a natural progression. My children's assumption of leadership roles was inevitable, and while it may have caused friction in the short term, it was a necessary step for the long-term growth and success of the business.

While leadership amongst family in business together is a natural progression, another concern I had was trying to protect my children from a feeling of forced involvement. I had known friends in my youth who had resented their family business involvement and I didn't want the same for my family. I wanted them to feel empowered and enjoy this lifestyle, while feeling they had choices about their individual futures. I encouraged them to take on other jobs locally, for comparison, and as they inevitably expanded their own entrepreneurial interests over the years I hoped they would feel supported and championed for their various projects and undertakings.

I also realized the importance of creating a culture that respects youth and values leadership capabilities, regardless of age. Age bias would not be tolerated, and having difficult conversations with employees who struggled to accept leadership from younger individuals became a priority.

Furthermore, the experience prompted us to work towards creating a collaborative team environment with a flat hierarchy, as much as possible. We emphasized the importance of delegation as an opportunity for inspiring leadership, thereby empowering all team members to take on leadership roles in various capacities.

As we moved forward, we implemented these valuable lessons in the business, and it brought about a positive shift in the company culture. The experience prepared us for the next iteration of our original teen years dilemma - the inclusion of our grandchildren in the business. With a clearer understanding of how to navigate the transition of leadership within a family business, we were better equipped to support the younger generation as they grew up within our company.

Today, our family business thrives with a collaborative and supportive team environment, where youth is respected, leadership is valued, and every member is suitably empowered to expand their roles as the opportunity arises. As we confidently look to the future, we hope that the next generation will seamlessly transition into leadership positions, continuing the legacy of our family business with strength and resilience.

Maintain a focus on lifestyle design as you continue vividly visioning the future for your family. Vision forward! And always have Fun!

Congratulations on reaching this important stage in your family business journey! In this chapter, we will explore the essential steps to create a positive and empowering work environment that fosters collaboration among family members and employees. By mastering these steps, you will be able to build a strong, cohesive team that is dedicated to the success of your family business.

Cultivate A Positive Company Culture And Team Dynamics.

To begin, it's crucial to establish a positive company culture that promotes trust, respect, and open communication. This can be achieved by setting a clear vision and values for your family business, and ensuring that everyone is aligned with these principles. Encourage teamwork and unity by organizing team-building activities and social gatherings to strengthen relationships among family members and employees.

Lead by example as the entrepreneur and business owner. Your actions and behaviors will set the tone for the company culture, so make sure to always act with integrity, kindness, and professionalism. Show appreciation for team members, recognize their hard work, and create an environment where everyone feels valued and supported.

Effective communication is crucial for promoting a positive company culture. Encourage open and honest dialogue, listen to your team members' ideas and concerns, and provide regular feedback to ensure that everyone feels heard and understood. As team members come forward with ideas and suggestions make sure to let them know you have received these. It's really important to give them feedback about their input, especially as it relates to how you might be willing or unwilling to utilize or implement their suggestions. If you don't plan to take action on their ideas, it's respectful and usually of interest to the contributor to know why their input may not be workable, or useful. Perhaps you've tried it before, etc. This will not only help the employee realize their input has not fallen on deaf ears, it will also help build trust and transparency, creative positivity and collaboration at work. In this day of global travel and work visas, sometimes employees may be accustomed to a different work environment in their home culture and may feel their input may benefit your family business, even though how they do things at home may be significantly different from what you have envisioned, or created. It can be difficult, sometimes, for team members to understand why you may not be eager to pivot in the direction that may be more familiar to them. If you're transparent about your response, perhaps you'll ruffle feathers but you may also foster a deeper respect for difference. Regardless of the outcome, it's respectful to thank employees for their genuine interest and desire to positively contribute to business improvement.

In terms of team dynamics, it's important to foster a sense of unity and camaraderie among your employees and family members. Establish clear roles and responsibilities, and create opportunities for everyone to contribute their unique skills and talents to the business. Encourage collaboration and cooperation, and empower your team to work together towards common goals.

Furthermore, promoting a positive team dynamic also means addressing and resolving conflicts in a proactive and constructive manner. Encourage healthy debates and discussions, and provide support and resources for conflict resolution when needed. By creating a safe and respectful environment for addressing issues, you can prevent toxic behaviors and build a strong and cohesive team.

Remember that as your company gains momentum and longevity, the hiring practices of your family business will strengthen. Enough can't be said about implementing great hiring practices as a means toward fostering a positive team dynamic and healthy workplace. In time, you will have a fairly well established understanding of your family business culture. Taking the time and making the effort, to do what you can to create a "good fit" between your team and a new hire, can save a lot of future grief or difficult terminations.

Ultimately, a positive company culture and strong team dynamics can significantly impact the success and sustainability of your family business. By fostering an environment of trust, respect, and collaboration, you can enhance employee satisfaction, improve productivity, and create a foundation for long-term growth and success.

In conclusion, as a beginner entrepreneur with a vision to establishing a thriving family busines, cultivating a positive company culture and promoting strong team dynamics is crucial for your success. By setting a clear vision and values, leading by example, fostering open communication, and promoting teamwork, you can create a supportive and collaborative work environment that will benefit both your employees and your bottom line. Embrace the opportunity to shape the culture and dynamics of your business, and watch as it flourishes into a thriving and successful venture.

Establish Clear Communication Channels And Regular Family Business Meetings.

Effective communication is the backbone of any successful business. Implement communication tools such as Slack, Microsoft Teams, or Zoom to streamline internal communication and ensure that everyone is on the same page. Additionally, schedule regular family business meetings to discuss important matters, share updates, and address any concerns. These meetings are an opportunity to maintain transparency and involve all members in decision-making processes. From team collaboration to client satisfaction, here are 9 communication strategies for family entrepreneurs, that will help keep the family business strong, including a few pointers about how communication impacts business outcomes:

1. **Regular family business meetings:** Schedule weekly or monthly family meetings to discuss important family matters and decisions. This will ensure that everyone is on the same page and provide a platform for open communication.

2. **Define roles and responsibilities:** Clearly outline each family member's roles and responsibilities within the family business to avoid any confusion or overlap of duties.

3. **Use technology:** Utilize communication tools such as email, messaging apps, or virtual meetings to stay connected with family members who may not be physically present.

4. **Set clear goals:** Establish and communicate clear goals and objectives for the family business, ensuring that everyone understands the direction in which the business is headed.

5. **Provide regular updates:** Keep family members informed about the performance and progress of the family business through regular updates and reports.

6. **Create a feedback loop:** Encourage open and honest feedback from family members about the family business, allowing for constructive discussions and improvements.

7. **Address conflicts:** Establish clear channels for conflict resolution within the family business to ensure that any disagreements or misunderstandings are addressed promptly and effectively.

8. **Celebrate achievements:** Recognize and celebrate the achievements of family members within the business, fostering a positive and supportive work environment.

9. **Seek professional assistance:** Consider hiring a professional mediator or facilitator to help facilitate communication and hold effective family business meetings.

Foster A Supportive And Collaborative Work Environment.

Create an atmosphere where everyone feels valued and supported. Model collaboration and idea-sharing by providing a platform for family and team members to contribute their thoughts and suggestions. Emphasize the importance of working together towards a common goal, and recognize the unique strengths and contributions of each team member.

- Clearly define the vision and values of the family business to foster a supportive and collaborative work environment.

- Establish open and transparent communication channels to encourage feedback and ideas from all family members involved in the business.

- Create a flexible work schedule that accommodates the needs of individual family members while ensuring productivity and efficiency.

- Implement regular team-building activities and workshops to strengthen bonds and encourage collaboration among family members.

- Establish clear roles and responsibilities for each family member involved in the business to avoid misunderstandings and conflicts.

- Encourage a culture of continuous learning and personal development to support the growth and well-being of each family member in the business.

- Provide opportunities for family members to contribute their unique skills and talents to the business, fostering creativity and innovation in the family work environment.

Provide Ongoing Training And Professional Development Opportunities.

Invest in the growth and development of your team by offering training and professional development opportunities. Websites like Udemy, Kajabi, Coursera, or LinkedIn Learning offer a wide range of courses that can help your employees enhance their skills and knowledge. By investing in their growth, you not only empower your team but also strengthen the capabilities of your family business.

When onboarding a team member for HR who has little previous experience but the right personality, it's prudent to ensure a minimum of compliance training, especially when there are compliance obligations to be met. HR is an example where awareness of labour relations regulations will be paramount.

Another example would be any situation of family members growing up in a family business who will necessarily need to become familiar with tasks and roles that are new to them, or for which they do not have requisite training. At minimum, help them get moderately up to speed by the time they are needed to have team oversight.

Recognize And Reward Individual And Team Achievements.

Acknowledge the hard work and dedication of your team members by implementing an employee recognition program, or a system of rewards. Platforms such as Bonusly or Kazoo provide a framework for recognizing individual and team achievements, fostering a sense of appreciation and motivation within the team. You can also implement an in-house system of rewards, such as team member discounts on shop products or services, promotional item give-aways, accumulation of points for redemption tied to high achievement, or other incentivization programs.

Address And Resolve Conflicts Promptly Through Open Dialogue.

Conflicts are inevitable, but how they are handled can make a significant impact on your business. Encourage open dialogue and proactive resolution of conflicts within the team. Encourage family members to actively listen to one another's perspectives and concerns, and to seek to understand before being understood. Clearly define the conflict. Ensure that everyone involved understands the nature of the conflict and the specific issues at hand. It's important to actively listen to all parties involved in the conflict, allowing each person to express their thoughts and feelings without interruption.

State the specific ground rules at the start of a dialogue. One person at a time has the floor. While they have the floor no one else speaks. One person briefly states their position in a dialogue related to a conflict, as person #2 listens. After #1 is complete #2 has to repeat back to #1 everything they said until person #1 is satisfied they're hearing back a match to their intention, plus a match to their perspective. The receiver doesn't acknowledge agreement or disagreement. The intention is merely to allow each person to be fully heard. The mediator just keeps tabs on keeping to the communication guidelines. Next, positions are reversed. No resolution is intended. After each perspective has been carefully aired and is complete this phase is complete. Finally, suggestions for compromise can be offered.

Both parties can be encouraged to brainstorm and generate potential solutions to the conflict, considering the pros and cons of options. Collaboratively exploring various solutions can lead to more effective resolutions.

If a resolution has been agreed upon, establish clear next steps and responsibilities for all parties involved. This can help prevent future misunderstandings and ensure that the resolution is implemented effectively. If a conflict has not reached resolution, consider investing in conflict resolution training programs or mediation services to equip your team with the skills needed to navigate and resolve conflicts effectively.

By incorporating these strategies, you can create a vibrant and supportive work culture that empowers your family members and employees, fosters collaboration, and strengthens the foundation of your family business. Remember, a positive and collaborative work environment is essential for the long-term success of your family business.

Resources:

- Communication tools such as Slack or Microsoft Teams for team communication

- Employee engagement software like Officevibe or TinyPulse

- Training and development resources from Udemy, Coursera, or LinkedIn Learning

- Employee recognition platforms such as Bonusly or Kazoo

- Conflict resolution training programs or mediation services

Best of luck as you move into the next family business building phase. Remember to work toward building a culture of empowerment and collaboration in your family business!

Chapter Summary

> ➤ Cultivate a positive company culture and team dynamics by establishing clear values and vision, encouraging teamwork, and organizing team-building activities.

> ➤ Establish clear communication channels and regular family business meetings to ensure transparency and involvement in decision-making processes.

> Foster a supportive and collaborative work environment by encouraging idea-sharing, providing ongoing training and professional development opportunities, and recognizing and rewarding individual and team achievements.

> Address and resolve conflicts promptly through open dialogue and proactive resolution.

> Invest in communication tools, employee engagement software, training and development resources, employee recognition platforms, and conflict resolution training programs or mediation services to support the creation of a positive and collaborative work environment.

Chapter FAQ

Question: *How can I foster a supportive and collaborative work environment within my family business?*

Answer: You can foster a supportive and collaborative work environment by encouraging collaboration and idea-sharing, providing a platform for employees to contribute their thoughts and suggestions, and emphasizing the importance of working together towards a common goal. Recognize the unique strengths and contributions of each team member to create a sense of value and support within the team.

Question: What are some examples of team-building activities I can organize for my family business team?

Answer: Team-building activities can include off-site retreats, outdoor adventure activities, or workshops focused on teamwork and communication. Additionally, social gatherings such as company dinners or team outings can help strengthen relationships among family members and employees.

Question: What are the benefits of establishing a culture of empowerment and collaboration in my family business?

Answer: Establishing a culture of empowerment and collaboration can lead to increased employee engagement, improved teamwork, higher productivity, and a positive work environment. It can also contribute to the long-term success and sustainability of your family business.

Family Business Fortune Telling: Predicting Succession And Growth For The Long Haul

This chapter will help you:

- Understand the importance of setting long-term goals for sustainable growth and expansion of your family business.

- Recognize the crucial role of accumulating profits for reinvestment and diversification in ensuring the longevity of your business.

- Identify the process of identifying and preparing potential successors within the family for leadership positions.

- Understand the significance of developing a formal succession plan to ensure a smooth transition of the business to the next generation.

- Recognize the value of seeking professional advice for wealth management and legacy planning to secure the financial future of your family business.

Resources:

- Business planning software for long-term goal setting

- Investment and wealth management tools

- Succession planning resources

- Estate planning and legacy management services from financial advisors or lawyers

Lessons Learned: The Emotional, Spiritual, And Financial Transformation Of A Family Business Founder

I never imagined that my journey to create an ideal family lifestyle as a family business founder in a small island town, would be filled with so much emotional turmoil, but that's the thing about life - it's full of unexpected twists and turns. As I look back on the past 40 years, I realize just how much my family and business have shaped me into the person I am today.

My son and daughter have been my business partners from the very beginning, and together, we built something truly special. Our family business was not just about making profits, it was about creating an ideal family lifestyle and fostering a deep love and connection between us. We poured our hearts and souls into our work, and it showed. Our business flourished, and this year we celebrate our 40th anniversary with pride and joy.

However, as with all families and businesses, conflicts arise. A couple of years ago I made a difficult decision that snowballed. I fired an employee who was not performing according to the terms of her hire. Little did I know that this decision would be one of the catalysts for a chain of disagreements that would test the very foundation of our family and business.

This conflict occurred when my business partners were furious about a decision made without their consultation. Initially, I was genuinely surprised and wouldn't have imagined they wouldn't have had confidence in my decision. Just another example of how sometimes, we can be so wrong! They felt that I had overstepped and when I tried to view through their lens it was not a stretch to understand what they were feeling. However, hindsight is not helpful in these circumstances. Even though I stayed 100% accountable to my decision via a full-time commitment to doing the job myself again, until I had a much better bookkeeping team structure implemented, the damage was done. The snowball gathered size and momentum as it tumbled downhill!

And then I was blindsided by an event, and the snowball tumbled faster. A family succession plan had been crafted for my kids, without my knowledge or approval, by a team of former business accountants. I guess they assumed, over the course of years, that the plan wouldn't require discussion. It had been crafted partially for the purpose of preparing to respond to a regulatory requirement dictating dissolution of a trust agreement after a specific number of years. As that deadline hurtled toward us with alarming speed, I found myself being handed a preconceived succession plan which felt as if it landed practically out of nowhere. I felt betrayed and hurt. On our journey through decades, the hard work, connection and inspiration became blurry, and I confused. I struggled to get my bearings, not knowing how to respond, only knowing that I absolutely had to respond because a deadline was fast approaching. Sadly, my responses were unskillful and misunderstood. That snowball was scary big by now.

As the year went on, tensions ran high, and the trust dissolution meetings with tax accountants and lawyers only added fuel to the fire. The atmosphere within our once tight-knit family business became one of discomfort and distrust, and I know we all felt the weight of the world on our shoulders. The dissolution decisions were on me as the trustee, and the pressure felt close to unbearable. All three of us suffered through this gruelling trial by fire.

Despite the turmoil, one thing became abundantly clear - my family came first. No matter what challenges we faced, I was willing to do whatever it took to mend the rift that had formed between us. We all experienced a year of emotional and physical pain and through it all, we aimed to stand by each other, and tried mightily to weather the storm together.

As the deadline for the trust dissolution loomed, I knew that I had to make a decision. It wasn't an easy task, but I navigated through the murky waters of family and business to make the best choice for all of us. We may have experienced a challenging year, but we emerged on the other side, battered and bruised, yet stronger and more resilient than ever.

Looking back, I realized that the journey we had been on was one of transformation. From a poverty mindset to a mindset of prosperity and abundance, we had grown and learned so much along the way. We may have lost material things, but we never lost sight of the most important thing - our family. Love, I came to understand, is the opening door to healing and reconciliation.

As I reflect on everything that has transpired, I am filled with gratitude for the lessons learned. I believe that all things happen for a reason, and I am grateful for the wisdom and strength that this journey has bestowed upon me. I have grown emotionally, financially, and spiritually, and I am ready to face whatever the future may hold. I hope that by sharing my story, I can offer hope and inspiration to others who may be facing similar challenges, and especially those beginner entrepreneurs who dream of creating an ideal family lifestyle while building a successful family business. After all, love may be the binding force that holds us together in the end. No matter the challenges that lie ahead, with love and unwavering determination, anything is possible. You can replace stuff, but you can't replace family, and the journey of transformation is one that is both rewarding and life-changing. Remember, all things happen for a reason, and with a grateful heart, anything is possible.

Stay grateful and have Fun!

Congratulations on reaching this stage in your journey to creating a successful family business! In this chapter, we will delve into the essential steps for predicting succession and growth for the long haul.

Plan For Sustainable Growth And Succession

The key to long-term success for your family business lies in planning for sustainable growth and efficient succession. Setting long-term goals for your business will provide you with a clear roadmap for expansion. For example, you may set a goal to expand your family business into new geographical areas or to introduce new product lines within a certain timeframe.

As a beginner entrepreneur, **it's crucial to understand the importance of setting long-term goals** for sustainable growth and expansion of your family business. Setting long-term goals lays the foundation for strategic planning and decision-making. These goals can help you prioritize tasks, allocate resources, and make informed choices that will benefit your business in the long run. While it may be tempting to focus solely on short-term gains, setting long-term goals can help guide the direction and vision for the future. By establishing these goals, you are setting the stage for sustainable growth and helping to ensure the success of your family business for years to come. A clear roadmap can take you from where your business is now to where you want your business to be in the future, enabling you to make more informed decisions and achieve those long-term goals.

Furthermore, setting long-term goals can help you stay focused and motivated, even during challenging times. It's easy to get caught up in the day-to-day operations of your business, but by keeping your long-term goals in mind, you can maintain a sense of purpose and drive. This can help you and your family business overcome obstacles and push through tough times, knowing that your efforts are contributing to the larger goal of sustainable growth and expansion. Probably, there'll be times when you'll need to pivot, and by having an eye to the future over the long term, you'll become more mentally prepared for flexibility, fluidity and ideas for potential pivot paths.

In addition, having long-term goals in place can also help you attract and retain top talent for your family business. When prospective employees see that your business has a clear vision for the future and is committed to long-term success, they are more likely to feel confident and secure in joining your team. Similarly, existing employees will feel more invested in the success of the business when they understand the long-term goals and how their work contributes to achieving them.

Ultimately, setting long-term goals for your family business is about laying the groundwork for a successful and thriving enterprise. By taking the time to define your long-term goals, you can set your business on a path for sustainable growth and expansion. So, take the time to reflect on where you want your family business to be in the future, and start setting those long-term goals today. Your efforts will not only benefit the future of your business but also inspire and motivate others to join you on this journey.

As a beginner entrepreneur, **it's vital to understand the importance of accumulating profits for reinvestment and diversification.** It's another crucial aspect of building a successful business and ensuring its long-term sustainability. Reinvest your profits back into your business to fund expansion initiatives, hire new talent, or invest in technology to stay competitive in the market. Diversifying your investments helps minimize risks by spreading investments across different sectors or markets. **Diversification is a key feature of creating wealth.** Diversification positions you for future growth and success.

Understanding the value of a diversified investment portfolio can be more than beneficial for an entrepreneur undertaking the exciting adventure of creating wealth via a family business. It serves as a successful long term business strategy to shield your hard-earned profits from unexpected changes in the marketplace and can be a source of recovery for rebuilding after unexpected downturns, setbacks and losses. Setting the wheels of a regular reinvestment of profits program in motion, means greater attunement to changes in the financial climate and optimum positioning to take advantage of new opportunities for financial advancement.

When you accumulate profits for reinvestment, you are essentially putting money back into your business to fuel its growth. This can take many forms, such as investing in new products or services, expanding your operations, or upgrading your facilities and equipment. By reinvesting your profits, you are making a commitment to the future success of your business and ensuring that it remains competitive in the marketplace.

One important aspect of reinvestment is investing in technology. In today's digital age, technology plays a crucial role in the success of any business. By investing in new technologies, you can streamline your operations, improve efficiency, and stay ahead of the competition. Whether it's upgrading your software systems, implementing new automated processes, or investing in cutting-edge machinery, consistent investments in upgrading or implementing new technology can have a significant impact on your business performance.

All of these aspects demonstrate how diversifying your family business is a key component of accumulating profits for reinvestment. **Diversification involves expanding your business into new products, services, or markets to reduce risk and create new opportunities for growth.** By diversifying, you help protect your business from economic downturns or shifts in consumer preferences while also maximizing your potential for success.

As you position your business for long-term success, you want to have a strategic plan in place for reinvesting profits and diversifying your business. Think about conducting thorough market research, analyzing your financials, and seeking the advice of industry professionals to make informed decisions.

All of this requires discipline and a long-term mindset. It's important to resist the temptation to take all the profits out of your business and instead reinvest a portion back into the business for growth. This approach will enable you to build a strong foundation for your business and create opportunities for it to thrive in the future.

By reinvesting your profits and diversifying your business, you are also sending a message to your customers, employees, and stakeholders that you are committed to the long-term success of your business. This can help build trust and loyalty, which can be invaluable in building a sustainable business.

Remember to approach reinvestment and diversification with a strategic mindset and seek the advice of professionals when making important decisions. With the right approach, you can build a strong and sustainable business that can withstand the test of time.

Identifying potential successors within the family for leadership positions is a critical step in ensuring a smooth transition of the business to the next generation. This involves **assessing the skills and interests of family members and providing them with the necessary training and experience to prepare them for leadership roles in the future.**

There is a **frequently overlooked aspect** of this critical step that could profoundly impact you as a beginner family business entrepreneur and the sustainability of your company well into the future, if you take the time to give it serious consideration. **Are you planning to spend the bulk of your time working in your business, or on your business?** Planning is a key word because, of course, it's often imperative for beginner entrepreneurs to spend the formative business years working in their business, unless they're starting from a position of financial security. As that's not likely to be the bulk of people starting out on this entrepreneurial journey, it's important for those who want to gain financial independence to take heed as you formulate your vivid vision of your future.

When you only work in your business, you are a lone ranger and by definition, indispensable. If you are growing a new business with family members only, then you will have to be laser focused on ensuring that every family member involved will be trained, and at least minimally competent in carrying out most of the roles and tasks required for the day to day operations of your business. If you are creating team and only work in your business, for the most part you will be indispensable to your team. When the unexpected happens, who will keep the business running?

When you start and sustain a family business, you are demonstrating your entrepreneurial nature. Hopefully, the family members that grow the business with you will have, or take on the entrepreneurial spirit and characteristics. Remember, entrepreneurship is not everyone's path. Your team depends on your leadership not only for fortitude but for ideas, inspiration and flexibility. If you want a sustainable family business, it cannot depend on you. It's a concept that must be perpetuated and communicated to incoming family members joining the team. You need to inspire leadership in others and be satisfied with working mostly on your business, as your team grows and you have people in place to carry daily operations forward. This is business sustainability. Families need to understand the concept of longevity, sustainability, and the ability to pivot when necessary. Family members all need awareness and understanding of the difference between working in, and working on the family business, and senior members should serve as role models for incoming generations.

Developing a formal succession plan involves outlining the process and timeline for transitioning the leadership of the business to the next generation. This plan should address key aspects such as leadership roles, ownership transfer, decision-making processes, and conflict resolution mechanisms. As in everything else in business and life, **it's**

important to never think of formal plans as set in stone. Stay focused on the need for fluidity, flexibility and potential pivot paths.

Seeking professional advice for wealth management and legacy planning may provide valuable guidance in securing the financial future of your family business. Wealth managers, financial advisors, and lawyers specialized in estate planning can assist you in structuring your assets, minimizing tax liabilities, and ensuring the smooth transfer of wealth to the next generation. It's also important to remember that while others can offer advice and guidance, ultimately you need to know and understand your business thoroughly and have the competency to assess and weigh the validity and helpfulness of the advice being offered. For your family business to extract maximum benefit from future planning make sure all key players and decision-makers are kept up to date, be prepared to revise and review and stay creatively connected.

Now it's your turn to create your ideal lifestyle. My intention for you as you embark on this exciting and challenging family journey with your loved ones is that you have fun inside of a powerful, creative, learning experience and the realization of all your best dreams. May you be filled with gratitude and prosper.

Resources:

To aid you in setting long-term goals, business planning software such as Enloop can be incredibly helpful in creating detailed and comprehensive business plans that outline your growth strategies.

When it comes to investment and wealth management, tools like Betterment (Canada) or Robinhood (U.S.) can provide you with the necessary resources and support to manage and grow your assets effectively.

For succession planning, resources from the Family Business Institute can provide valuable insights and templates to help you develop a structured plan for the future leadership of your business.

Finally, for estate planning and legacy management, professional services from financial advisors and lawyers specializing in this area can offer expert guidance and support to secure the long-term legacy of your family business.

With these essential steps and resources, you are better prepared for the succession and growth of your family business for the long haul. Helpful planning and professional advice can help set the foundation for a successful and sustainable family business for generations to come.

Chapter Summary

➢ Plan for sustainable growth and succession with long-term goals and reinvestment of profits

➢ Identify potential successors within the family and develop a formal succession plan

➢ Seek professional advice for wealth management and legacy planning

➢ Utilize business planning software such as Enloop for goal setting

➢ Utilize resources from the Family Business Institute for succession planning templates and guidance

Chapter FAQ

Question: How can diversification of the family business help minimize risks?

Answer: Diversifying the family business across different sectors or markets can help minimize risks by spreading investments and revenue streams. For example, if one sector experiences a downturn, the family business can rely on the revenues from other diversified sectors to mitigate the impact. This helps in creating a more stable and resilient business in the long run.

Question: *Why is it crucial to accumulate profits for reinvestment and diversification?*

Answer: It is crucial to accumulate profits for reinvestment and diversification because it allows the family business to fund expansion initiatives, hire new talent, or invest in technology to stay competitive in the market. Reinvesting profits back into the business can also help in diversifying the business across different sectors or markets which can minimize risks and create sustainable growth.

Question: *How can seeking professional advice for wealth management and legacy planning help secure the financial future of the family business?*

Answer: Seeking professional advice for wealth management and legacy planning can provide valuable guidance in structuring assets, minimizing tax liabilities, and ensuring the smooth transfer of wealth to the next generation. Wealth managers, financial advisors, and lawyers specialized in estate planning can offer expert support in managing and growing the family business's assets effectively.

Conclusion

Congratulations on finishing the "Family Business Blueprint"! You've just taken a gigantic leap towards creating a successful family business and laying the foundation for a generational legacy of financial freedom and creative family collaboration. Just start where you are.

Starting a family business can be an incredibly rewarding experience. I currently enjoy shared ownership of three companies with my 2 adult children. This is a life not without its challenges. You may be feeling excited and inspired, but you might also be feeling a little overwhelmed and unsure of where to start. That's completely normal, and I want you to know that you are not alone. You're not growing unless you're outside of your comfort zone. And starting a new business usually takes us outside of our comfort zone. I've founded multiple companies over the years and it's usually with a mix of fear and excitement. I don't know what it will be for you but if you've read this all the way to this conclusion chapter then you must have a desire and vision inside of you that's waiting to be fulfilled. *You are magnificent and you can do it!* With the right mindset and the practical advice and strategies that you've just learned from this book, you can absolutely create the family business of your dreams.

Throughout the book, you've learned about the importance of financial freedom, the power of creative family collaboration, and the significance of creating a lifestyle legacy. You've been given practical advice, tips, tricks, and real-life examples to help you navigate the world of family business. It's all been laid out for you, and now it's time to take action.

I encourage you to start implementing the steps outlined in the "Family Business Blueprint" right away. Don't wait for the perfect moment or for everything to feel just right. Take action now, and keep going until you're ready to open the doors of your new family business. Remember, it's okay to start small and grow from there. The important thing is to keep moving forward and stay committed to your vision.

As you embark on this exciting journey, don't forget to prioritize family communication and collaboration. Keep the lines of communication open, and be willing to listen to each other's ideas and concerns. Embrace creativity and innovation, and use them to your advantage as you *have fun working together towards your shared goals.*

Finally, never lose sight of your lifestyle legacy. Create a business that not only supports you and your family financially, but also aligns with your values, passions, and desired lifestyle. This is what will truly set your family business apart and make it a sustainable and fulfilling venture for generations to come.

It's time to go out there and make it happen. Take this "Family Business Blueprint" with your own accumulated wisdom and this new found knowledge and take step by step action. Focus! Prepare! Action!

Introducing Liz Zed

Liz Zed, Phd, MCC The Mastermind Behind The Blueprint For Family Business Success

Are you an aspiring entrepreneur dreaming of an ideal family lifestyle and financial independence? Your guide is here and it's called "Family Business Blueprint", the latest book from Liz Zed.

Liz wrote this book because she's experienced first-hand the struggles, challenges, and rewards of starting and growing a family business. Liz is on a mission to help entrepreneurs like you achieve success in the family business realm.

Liz Zed's expertise in counseling and coaching, combined with her extensive entrepreneurial experience, makes her uniquely qualified to help the beginner entrepreneur start and grow a family business. It also makes her the perfect mentor for those seeking to combine financial success with a strong family connection and an ideal lifestyle.

So, if you're ready to be inspired, energized, and equipped with the knowledge and actions needed to kickstart your family business journey, start reading "Family Business

Blueprint" right now. Liz Zed's practical advice and empowering insights will set you on the path to achieving your entrepreneurial dreams.

She understands the challenges and rewards of running a family business and wants to help others achieve the same success and fulfillment.

Liz Zed crafted this blueprint for family business to empower an aspiring business owner with the knowledge, inspiration, and actionable steps necessary to build a successful and fulfilling enterprise that spans generations.

Liz is an expert guide who has hands-on experience in founding businesses, including co-owning multiple companies with her own family. Her love of coaching and extensive business coaching expertise, has inspired and empowered hundreds of beginner entrepreneurs in achieving lifestyle and business goals that align with their top values and aspirations.

Coaching With Liz

- Family Business Blueprint Implementation & Action

- Your top values guiding your goal-setting

- Uncover ambivalence holding you back from manifesting your heart's desires

- Raising your vibrational level & connecting with your higher Self

- Money Mindset & the 365 Day Prosperity Plan

- Business Building Booster Sessions

You can contact Liz Zed directly by booking a complimentary coaching consultation at FamilyBusinessBlueprint.ca